Astrology Activated:

Cutting Edge Insight Into the Ancient Art of Astrology (Understanding Zodiac Signs and Horoscopes)

By: Serra Night

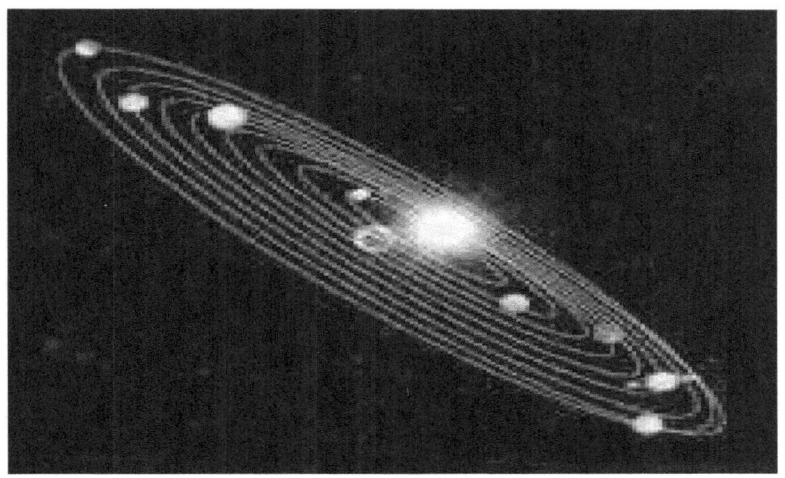

Copyright 2019 by Serra Night - All rights reserved.

This content is provided with the sole purpose of providing relevant information on a specific topic for which every reasonable effort has been made to ensure that it is both accurate and reasonable. Nevertheless, by purchasing this content you consent to the fact that the author, as well as the publisher, are in no way experts on the topics contained herein, regardless of any claims as such that may be made within. As such, any suggestions or recommendations that are made within are done so purely for entertainment value. It is recommended that you always consult a professional prior to undertaking any of the advice or techniques discussed within.

This is a legally binding declaration that is considered both valid and fair by both the Committee of Publishers Association and the American Bar Association and should be considered as legally binding within the United States.

The reproduction, transmission, and duplication of any of the content found herein, including any specific or extended information will be done as an illegal act regardless of the end form the information ultimately takes. This includes copied versions of the work both physical, digital and audio unless expressed consent of the Publisher is provided beforehand. Any additional rights reserved.

Furthermore, the information that can be found within the pages described forthwith shall be considered both accurate and truthful when it comes to the recounting of facts. As such, any use, correct or incorrect, of the provided information will render the Publisher free of responsibility as to the actions taken outside of their direct purview. Regardless, there are zero scenarios where the original author or the Publisher can be deemed liable in any fashion for any damages or hardships that may result from any of the information discussed herein.

Additionally, the information in the following pages is intended only for informational purposes and should thus be thought of as universal. As befitting its nature, it is presented without assurance regarding its prolonged validity or interim quality. Trademarks that are mentioned are done without written consent and can in no way be considered an endorsement from the trademark holder.

Table of Contents

INTRODUCTION 1

HOW TO GET THE MOST OUT OF THIS BOOK 2

CHAPTER 1: THE CELESTIAL BODIES — THE PLANETS EXPLAINED 4

    The Creation of the Zodiac 4
    How the Celestial Bodies Affect Astrology 5
    The Sun 5
    The Moon 6
    Mars 7
    Jupiter 7
    Saturn 8
    Mercury 9
    Venus 9
    Transcendental Planets 10
    Uranus 10
    Pluto 10
    Neptune 11
    The Astrological Wheel 12

CHAPTER 2: THE 12 SIGNS OF THE ZODIAC 14

    Aries (March 21-April 19) The Ram 15
    Taurus (April 20-May 21) The Bull 16
    Gemini (May 21-June 20) The Twins 18
    Cancer (June 21-July 22) The Crab 19
    Leo (July 23-August 22) The Lion 20
    Virgo (August 23-September 22) The Maiden 22
    Libra (September 23-October 22) The Scales 24
    Scorpio (October 23-November 21) The Scorpion 26
    Sagittarius (November 22-December 21) The Archer 27
    Capricorn (December 22-January 19) The Goat 28
    Aquarius (January 20-February 18) The Water Bearer 30
    Pisces (February 19-March 20) The Fish 32

CHAPTER 3: HOW TO READ YOUR NATAL CHART 35

    How to Find Your Sun Sign 35
    What the Houses Tell Us 37
    Locating the Ascendant 37
    The Astrological Houses Defined 37
    How the Planets Play a Part in the Natal Chart 39
    The Second Set of Planets Are Outer Planets 39
    Understanding and Interpreting Your Chart 40

CHAPTER 4: YOUR SUN SIGN AND YOU 42
Sun Signs in Astrology and Their Meaning 42

CHAPTER 5: HOW TO DETERMINE YOUR MOON SIGN 57
Moon in Aries 58
Moon in Taurus 58
Moon in Gemini 58
Moon in Cancer 59
Moon in Leo 59
Moon in Virgo 60
Moon in Libra 60
Moon and Scorpio 60
Moon in Sagittarius 61
Moon in Capricorn 61
Moon in Aquarius 62
Moon in Pisces 62

CHAPTER 6: YOUR RISING SIGN 65
Aries Ascendant 65
Taurus Ascendant 66
Gemini Ascendant 67
Cancer Ascendant 67
Leo Ascendant 68
Virgo Ascendant 69
Libra Ascendant 69
Scorpio Ascendant 70
Sagittarius Ascendant 71
Capricorn Ascendant 71
Aquarius Ascendant 72
Pisces Ascendant 73

CHAPTER 7: ARE YOU BORN ON A CUSP? 76
Aries-Taurus Cusp (April 17–23) — The Cusp of Power 76
Taurus-Gemini Cusp (May 17–23) — The Cusp of Energy 77
Gemini-Cancer Cusp (June 18–24) — The Cusp of Magic 78
Cancer-Leo Cusp (July 19–25) — The Cusp of Oscillation 79
Leo-Virgo Cusp (August 19–25) — The Cusp of Exposure 80
Virgo-Libra Cusp (September 19–25) — The Cusp of Beauty 81
Libra-Scorpio Cusp (October 19–25) — The Cusp of Drama 82
Scorpio-Sagittarius Cusp (November 18–24) — The Cusp of Revolution 83
Sagittarius-Capricorn Cusp (December 28–24) — The Cusp of Prophecy 84
Capricorn-Aquarius Cusp (January 17–23) — The Cusp of Mystery and Imagination 85
Aquarius-Pisces Cusp (February 15–21) — The Cusp of Sensitivity 86

PISCES-ARIES CUSP (MARCH 17–23) — THE CUSP OF REBIRTH 87

CHAPTER 8: ARE YOU COMPATIBLE? 89
LOVE SECRETS OF VENUS 89
VENUS IN ARIES 90
VENUS IN TAURUS 91
VENUS IN GEMINI 92
VENUS IN CANCER 93
VENUS IN LEO 94
VENUS IN VIRGO 95
VENUS IN LIBRA 96
VENUS IN SCORPIO 97
VENUS IN SAGITTARIUS 98
VENUS IN CAPRICORN 99
VENUS IN AQUARIUS 100
VENUS IN PISCES 101

CHAPTER 9: HOW TO READ YOUR DAILY HOROSCOPE 102
WHY DO PEOPLE READ THEIR HOROSCOPE? 102
HOW ARE HOROSCOPES CREATED? 103
THE CORRECT WAY TO READ YOUR HOROSCOPE 103
WHAT ABOUT YOUR SUN SIGN? 104

CHAPTER 10: THE EFFECT OF ASTROLOGY ON DIFFERENT RELIGIONS AND CULTURES 105
THE CHINESE ZODIAC 105
EFFECTS ON RELATIONSHIPS 105
RELIGION 106
OTHER COUNTRIES INFLUENCED BY THE CHINESE ZODIAC 107
MYTHOLOGY — RACING TO THE FINISH 107
HINDUISM ASTROLOGY 110
THE PRINCIPLE OF VEDIC ASTROLOGY 110
THE PREDICTIVE VEDIC ASTROLOGY 110

CONCLUSION 112

DESCRIPTION 113

Introduction

Greetings! You have made a wonderful decision purchasing *Astrology Activated: Cutting Edge Insight Into the Ancient Art of Astrology (Understanding Zodiac Signs and Horoscopes)*. Thank you for doing so.

Most people around the world have heard of astrology, and most people even know the basics of their astrology chart, but few have learned about the deeper mechanics of this ancient spiritual practice.

In short, astrology is the spiritual science of the motion and placement of the celestial bodies and how they determine things about us as spiritual beings and about our trajectory in life. This book will give beginners the tools they need not only to understand more about their own astrological makeup but also to learn how the behavior of the planets affects our world at large.

Today, astrology has been found to be used by people on almost a daily basis to give them guidance in their life to produce expectations about people's personalities and future events.

The following chapters will discuss all the elements involved in Astrology—the Sun and the planets that orbit around it and what effects they have on the signs they rule, the Houses of all the signs of the Zodiac, and their elements. Additionally, the natal chart, the Ascendant, and Moon signs and their impact on a person's chart are detailed.

There are plenty of books on this subject on the market; thanks again for choosing this one! Every effort was made to ensure it is full of as much useful information as possible. Please enjoy!

How to Get the Most Out of This Book

This book is written to work in a number of ways:

- Read this book in its entirety to enjoy the discoveries you will derive from the art of Astrology and learn how a natal chart is drawn, as well as how to find your Ascendant (rising sign) and the position of the Moon.
- Use this book as a guide to help you review and reread portions of it that may pertain to you, someone you know, or someone who is new in your life, especially if you and want to get an idea of who they are through their astrological Sun sign.
- To help you understand how to draw your natal chart, study where the planets were positioned at the time of your birth.
- Learn how to read your horoscope correctly and include the zodiac signs where your Ascendant and Moon are represented.

This book is written to be informative and instructional. Know that there are a number of variables affecting everyone's natal chart. The Zodiac sign that you are born under is where the Sun was positioned on the day of your birth.

Since your natal chart shows where the planets were when you were born, it will tell you the characteristics and tendencies that encompass who you are.

Astrology may be mysterious to some, but this book will shed some light on the subject. Also, this book is for you to enjoy!

The Planets

Chapter 1: The Celestial Bodies — The Planets Explained

The ancient origins of astrology were traced in 18th Century B.C. in Mesopotamia by the Babylonian civilization. Many of the first astronomers were found in this civilization, and they studied astronomy, complementing this study with astrology. The Babylonians are credited with astrology's creation.

The Babylonian's modern astronomical measurement of minutes and seconds are derived from their system of numbers, as well as the introduction of the concept of the zodiac. The astrological charts they created gave them the ability to predict the change of seasons and particular celestial events that recurred each year. Because of the combination of their astrological charts and planetary movements, astronomy and astrology were considered the same science for 2,000 years.

In the 4th century B.C., the Greeks were introduced to the Babylonian astrology. Through the studies of thinkers like Plato and Aristotle, astrology became a science that was highly regarded by the Greeks. In time, the Romans and Arabs adopted astrology. The names of the zodiac signs were given Roman names, which are still used today. The science of astrology expanded throughout the world

The Creation of the Zodiac

The Zodiac, meaning "circle of animals" in Greek, is believed to have begun in Egypt and then later embraced by the Babylonians. The early astrologers were aware that the Sun would return to its initial position after it traveled over 12 lunar cycles.

Twelve constellations were connected to the progression of the seasons. Each constellation was assigned names of persons and animals. For example, the rainy season in Babylonia would occur when a specific constellation housed the Sun. This constellation was named for the water-bearer, Aquarius. However, do not be confused. Aquarius is an air sign, not a water sign. Subdivided into four groups, the signs of the Zodiac are:

- Air Signs: Aquarius, Gemini, Libra

- Earth Signs: Capricorn, Taurus, Virgo

- Fire Signs: Aries, Leo, Sagittarius

- Water Signs: Cancer, Scorpio, Pisces

Each group is recorded into its own group of "houses" on a circle. The division of the 12 houses is based on the Earth's rotation on a daily basis and relating to the situations of finances, relationships, travel, and the like. Alternately, the 12 signs of the zodiac are divided based on the yearly rotation of the earth traveling around the sun. They pertain to characteristics and areas of life, e.g., Mercury is representative of communication, cleverness, and wit, while the Moon is associated with motherly instincts and emotions, etc. The Sun and the Moon are associated with only one zodiac sign; the planets have two zodiac signs that they effect.

During this time, Babylonian astrologers considered the Sun, Moon, Mars, Jupiter, Mercury, and Venus to carry very specific powers. For example, Mars had a red color and was believed to be identified with war and aggression. (American Federation of Astrologers, 2019)

How the Celestial Bodies Affect Astrology

The planets are the most significant carriers of the role and destiny of a person's horoscope. Each has its own impact and identification of where they are at the time of a person's birth. The planets nearest to Earth has the strongest impact, and the planets farthest from Earth, known as transcendent planets, have an impact on the person, as well as the cumulative events at the time of their birth.

The Sun

The Sun is the core body around which all the other planets rotate. It is the most significant figure of the Universe. In astrology, the Sun is considered the special, central planet, although it is a star. Known as the God of all celestial spheres, the Sun is the symbol of cosmic consciousness and intelligence.

At the moment of birth, the Sun is the core essence of who you are, our conscious mind in Astrology. It offers life energy, vitality and shines if it is well placed. Physical appearance, constitution, and health are especially affected and also about the way an individual presents themselves to others and the type of energy they carry. It could be one that is courageous, dignified, and strong or one that is weak and indulgent.

The Sun portrays one's self, the way of being in the world. It can serve on different degrees, both the higher self and the ego.

Leo is ruled by the Sun and exalted in Aries.

It is the only star that is closest to the Earth at 92.96 million miles.

The Sun is our ego. It also controls our inner child. It makes the final decisions and reasons out things. It is our adult. Our basic identity and self-realization are the Sun.

The Sun is what we are learning to be. It is significant to realize that the Sun is the representation of reason rather than instinct. It reflects the present or "today and now," whereas the Moon is about the past in our lives through emotions.

Day of the week - The day of the week associated with the Sun is Sunday. It is associated with the eastern side of the world. Gold, rubies, and gemstones red in hue are related to the Sun.

The Sun in the body – brain, heart, head, bones, throat, mouth, lungs, spleen, arteries, blood, and circulation

Sun in business – the strength of the Sun will give an individual ruled by its energy the ability to do their best in their endeavors and the charisma that will draw everyone around them in a professional arena.

The Moon

While the Sun is who you are and dictates the zodiac personality, the Moon has the second most significant effect on your horoscope. The ebbs and tides caused by the Moon are known to people, and the biggest part is caused by gravity.

The Moon is a natural satellite of the Earth and is about 238,900 miles away. It is significant to astrology because the Moon is representative of the feminine principle. This principle is the most subtle and finest part of every human.

The Moon is all about your emotions and inner mood. The Moon is the ruler of Cancer, exalted in Taurus and weak in Scorpio and Capricorn. Eastern astrologers believe the Moon to be the most significant entity in each horoscope interpretation and understanding because it is our inner emotional world, our soul.

The Sun sign is easily known based on the day and month of your birth. However, the Moon sign is calculated by your date of birth, the time you were born, and the place of your birth.

The Moon orbits the Earth once every 27.322 days and visits each sign of the zodiac during its orbit. The Moon remains approximately two days in each sign. So, if on the day of your birth is when the Moon is about to enter the next sign, your time of birth is necessary to give you an accurate placement of the Moon in your chart. Exact times of birth are always favorable to chart, but an approximation of the time of birth can give an astrologer enough information to determine your Moon sign.

Day of the week - The day of the week associated with the Moon is Monday; its colors are white and silver, the gemstones are moonstone and pearls, and the side of the world is Southwest.

Moon in the body - breasts, ovaries, uterus, abdominal pain, and several psychological disorders

The Moon in business – natural sciences, army, archeology, psychology, and poetry

Mars

Mars rules the sign of Aries and Scorpio. The irony of this planet is that it is responsible for our first breath of life and our last breath on our death. This is indicated through the beginning of the zodiac circle with Aries, the sign of the infant, and the end of life in the sign of Scorpio, the sign of death.

Mars is linked with self-assertion and confidence, sexuality, energy, aggression, strength, impulsiveness, and ambition. The planet oversees competitions, physical activities, and sports in general.

Mars was honored as the mythological Roman god of war responsible for war, fights, and destruction and whose symbol is a symbol of a spear and shield. The soil of Mars and the human blood hemoglobin are rich in iron, which is the reason both share the deep red color.

The orbit of Mars around the Sun is 687 days and spends approximately 57.25 days in each zodiac sign. It's the first planet whose orbit is outside the Earth's orbit and does not set along with the Sun.

Day of the week - The day of the week associated with Mars is Tuesday. It occupies the south side of the world, and red is the color of the planet.

Mars in the body – the head, muscles, genitals, and prostate

Mars in business – surgeon, butcher, chemist, technician, hairdresser, engineer, electrician, and everything that relates to heavy machinery, tools, and hard work

Jupiter

Jupiter, next to the Sun, is the greatest body of our planetary system. Jupiter rules Pisces and Sagittarius and is associated with expansion, growth, good fortune, and prosperity. It governs foreign and long-distance travel, wealth, big business, religion, higher education, and the law. The urge for exploration and freedom, gambling, and the love of a party is associated with this planet.

Jupiter's orbit around the sun takes 11.9 years and spends 361 days, almost an Earth's year, in each zodiac sign. It is usually the fourth brightest object in the sky behind the Sun, Moon, and Venus.

Day of the week - Thursday is associated with Jupiter.

Jupiter in the body – hips, gall bladder, pancreas, liver, and upper legs

Jupiter in business – publishing, professors, politics, sports, advertising, diplomacy, banking, transport, energy, shipbuilding, tourism, and seafaring

The Romance languages (French jeudi, Spanish jueves, and Italian giovedi)

Jupiter is related to the liberal art of geometry.

In ancient Roman mythology, Jupiter is a Roman god identical to Zeus, the supreme god of Greek mythology.

Saturn

Saturn is the planet that rules Capricorn. Saturn, in Roman mythology, is the god of crops, seeds, and agriculture. He is also the father and founder of civilizations and leader of titans, conformity, and social order.

In astrology, Saturn relates to precision, focus, ethics, nobility, civility, career, dedication, authority figures, stability, productiveness, hard lessons that are valuable, destiny structures, protective roles, balance, and karma (you reap what you sow). Saturn is also a part of the commitment, responsibility, and sense of duty. The rings of Saturn that surround and enclose the planet reflects the idea of the limits of human beings.

Saturn takes 29.5 years to orbit around the Sun and spends approximately 2.46 years in each zodiac sign. In ancient Roman society, Saturn was worshipped as the most important and highest god among all other deities. He also shared the same level of worship with Jupiter.

Day of the week – The day of the week associated with Saturn is Saturday, and its colors are black and every shade of gray. The gems it corresponds to are amethyst, onyx, and blue sapphire.

Saturn in the body – bones, hair, teeth, rheumatism, arthritis, gallstones, loss of hair, and bone fractures

Saturn in business – geology, construction, history, mining, architecture, forestry, justice, dentistry, agriculture, and state affairs

Mercury

The planet that is closest to the Sun, Mercury has a significant connection to it. Mercury is known as the messenger of the gods and is known for its swiftness and speed. It carries information from one person or level of existence to another.

Mercury is the ruler of both Gemini and Virgo and is exalted in Aquarius and is seen as our way of communicating and thinking.

The smallest planet in the Solar system is Mercury, and it is closest to the Sun at 35.98 million miles. Mercury is the planet of information and where our mind goes most of this life.

Mercury takes 88 days to orbit around the sun and only spends 7.33 days in each zodiac sign. This is the fastest orbit of any of the other planets.

Day of the week - The day of the week associated with Mercury is Wednesday. The gemstones that are governed by Mercury are emerald, peridot, green jade, tsavorite, chrome tourmaline, chrome diopside, and any other natural green gems.

Mercury in the body – lungs and nervous system

Mercury in business – languages, small business, sales, commercial, tourism, transport, accounting, printing industry, medicine, therapy, and job management

Venus

The most visible and brightest planet of the Solar system is Venus. Taurus and Libra are ruled by Venus. It is also exalted in Pisces.

In ancient Roman mythology, Venus is the goddess of beauty and love, and she is able to stir passions among the gods.

It rises and sets with the Sun and is known as the Morning star. This planet is particularly significant because of what it represents—the enjoyable and beautiful part of life that includes the excitement and desire for life, joy, pleasures, songs, love, the ability for people to love one another, and the ability to receive love. It is the dominance of the feminine.

The orbit of Venus around the Sun is 225 days and spends 18.75 days in each of the signs of the zodiac.

Day of the week – The day of the week associated with Venus is Friday. The colors are pink, white, and a mix of colors to exude colorfulness.

Venus in the body – skin, neck, reproductive organs, cheeks, and kidneys

Venus in business – art, fashion design, architecture, hair, and beauty, working with precious metals, jewelry, gems, decorative objects, and public affairs

Transcendental Planets

Uranus, Pluto, and Neptune are newly discovered planets. The last discovered planet was Pluto, which was seen in 1930.

Transcendental planets are significant in the natal business and common astrology.

Uranus

The astronomer William Herschel discovered Uranus in 1781. Attributed to the planet are eccentricity, originality, and unconventionality. The planet is always contrary to tradition, the old, archaic, and boring. Strong individuality and the ability to be completely different are awakened in an individual.

The October Revolution, the fall of the Bastille and other upheavals, the discovery of the steam locomotive, and the creation of the telegraphs and railways have occurred and are associated with Uranus.

Uranus is the co-ruler of Aquarius and exalted in the sign of Scorpio.

It takes 84 years for Uranus to circle the Zodiac. It is not visible to the naked eye.

Uranus in business – physics, nuclear physics, psychology, energy, cybernetics, internet, computers, telephones, aviation, electrical engineering, and engineering

Pluto

Originally known as Planet X, it was first searched by Percival Lowell, the mathematician, astronomer, and founder of the Lowell Observatory in Flagstaff, Arizona.

The first project initiating the search began in 1906. Before he could validate his search and confirm the discovery, Lowell died in 1916. The search for Planet X did not resume until 1929 by the then director of the Lowell Observatory, Melvin Sliefer. Sliefer teamed with Clyde Tombo, an astronomer from Kansas and spent the following year photographing the night sky, checking the photographs to detect if any of the photographed objects had moved from their place.

Pluto was officially discovered on February 18, 1930, and observed as a moving object on photographic plates that were taken a month earlier in January.

Additional photos of Planet X were sent to the Harvard College Observatory for review and confirmation of the moving object's existence.

After Planet X's discovery, thousands of proposed names for the planet were sent to the Lowell Observatory. Venice Bernie, a young schoolgirl in Oxford, England, suggested naming the planet Pluto after the Roman god of the underworld. Bernie spoke about it in a conversation with her grandfather. He, in turn, passed on the suggestion to Herbert Hall Turner, the director and astronomy professor at the University Observatory at Oxford, who then proposed the name to his colleagues in the United States.

The demonic and infernal system that led to the creation of concentration camps, slaughterhouses, and gas chambers came into being by the formation of the Third Reich almost immediately after the discovery of Pluto.

It takes 248 years to fully circle the Zodiac. It remains in each sign of the Zodiac between 15 and 26 years.

Pluto is the co-ruler of Scorpio and exalted in Leo. It is known to be the secret of life and death.

Pluto in business – criminology, politics, electronics, military science, banking, weapons, explosives pathology, underground construction, oil, psychotherapy, hypnosis, and computer technology

Neptune

The official discovery of Neptune was made by Johann Gottfried Galle in 1846 by the use of mathematic calculations of John Couch Adams and Urbain Le Verrier. This made the finding a British-French-German discovery. However, the first observer of this planet was the Italian astronomer Galileo Galilei in 1613.

Neptune is a blueish hued planet and was named after the Roman god of the sea.

The names of the planets were those of Roman gods, and the astronomers continued to name new planets using names in Roman mythology.

Neptune is the ruling planet of Pisces and exalted in Cancer, along with Jupiter.

It takes Neptune 165 years to orbit the Sun and spends 13.75 years in each zodiac sign.

Neptune in the body - affects the nervous system and self-confidence

Neptune in business – art theory, theology, oceanography, chemicals, oil, pharmaceuticals, cosmetics, the perfume tobacco industry, music industry, coffee, and tea production, hotels, rest homes, spiritual centers, and film industry

The Astrological Wheel

The astrological wheel is where a diagram can be drawn to reveal a person's horoscope. The wheel is like a clock, divided into the 12 segments of the zodiac and runs counterclockwise.

The planet aligns with each sign of the zodiac at the time of an individual's birth. Wherever the Sun is at the moment of birth is the astrological zodiac sign of the person, followed by where the Moon and the person's ascendant (rising sign) is.

The *natal chart* of each individual is a diagram of the relative positions of planets and signs of the zodiac at a specific time (at one's birth) for use by astrologers in inferring individual character and personality traits and in foretelling events in a person's life.

The next chapter will identify each of the 12 signs of the Zodiac and their basic personality traits.

Signs of the Zodiac

Chapter 2: The 12 Signs of the Zodiac

The four parts to astrology include the planets and their orbit around the Sun, the signs of the Zodiac, the houses, and the aspects. Astrology is looked upon by astrologers as a gel of elements that complement the merging of these elements that make up the Universe. These elements synchronize and intertwine with one another in small and large ways.

The apparent annual path of the Sun's motion is called the ecliptic. This is the celestial sphere as seen from Earth. The Sun appears to move around the Earth's spin axis, which is tilted at 23.5° and lends to the seasonal variations in the amount of sunlight the earth receives on the surface. The other planets, except for Pluto, also orbit the Sun in pretty much the same plane.

Eight degrees on either side of the ecliptic is where you'll find the Zodiac. Its frequency and vibration allow people to express their behavior differently; how they live and how they express themselves are different as well.

Understanding the character of an individual's birth by determining the Zodiac signs and the meaning of specific planets found in the precise Zodiac sign the individual is born under, gives an astrologer the ability to understand and create their natal chart accurately and authentically to read their fate.

Let's begin with the first sign of the Zodiac and work our way around the astrological wheel.

Aries (March 21-April 19) The Ram

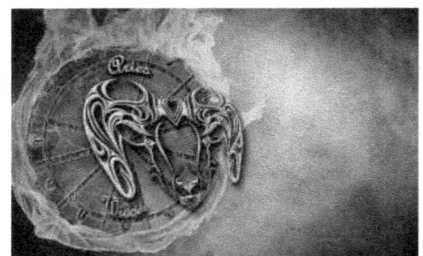

Zodiac Quality – Cardinal
Planet Ruler – Mars
Zodiac element - Fire
Gems – Diamonds, Coral and Amethyst

Aries is the Zodiac's first astrological sign. Its planetary ruler Mars makes Aries self-conscious, piercing, and courageous. People born under this sign sometimes overwork themselves.

Aries is indicative of dynamic, young, new, and animated. It is a cardinal sign with a fiery temperament. The sign is associated with the beginning of spring, a good time to begin new things.

Those born under the sign of Aries are determined, courageous, and passionate. They are good in leadership roles. Their temperament can reveal impatience and impulsiveness. They can be short-tempered and aggressive. As a Fire sign, Aries takes action, sometimes before mapping out a solid plan.

They may suffer from diseases of the head that can affect the blood vessels in the head and face. Migraines, neuralgia, insomnia, red cell problems and hair loss are indications of this type of condition.

Aries in business - Aries is an engineer, bricklayer, welder, new business, the beginning, a hairdresser.

Compatibility – Best with Leo, Sagittarius, Aquarius, and Gemini

Celebrated Aries – Lady Gaga, Robert Downey, Jr., Hugh Hefner, Elton John, Leonardo da Vinci, Vincent van Gogh, Jackie Chan, Mariah Carey, CJ So Cool

Taurus (April 20-MAY 21) The Bull

Zodiac Quality – Fixed
Planet Ruler – Venus
Zodiac Element – Earth
Gems – Sapphire, Emerald, and Alabaster

Taurus is practical, stable, devoted, responsible, and reliable. It is the second sign of the Zodiac. Those born under this sign have an abundance of patience. Since their sign is a bull, one may think they are aggressive. However, quite the opposite is true.

Taurus can be peaceful and methodical. They desire peace that can be brought with a stable marriage, job, and organized life. This is about pacifism, and there are no dark or heavy feelings. This is the area where Taurus finds joy, happiness, romance, fertility, the gift of music, and the inclination to possess beautiful things.

Taurus can be seen as a fixed sign with energy that can't be changed. They can be slow to change and not open to new things (this may be altered by their other planetary aspects). They usually need more time to fully understand the problem. They can be slow to learn, but once they do, they retain what they learn.

They are a fixed, feminine sign whose element is earth. This also represents the allure of spring, pleasure, and all sorts of comfort. They desire a comfortable, pleasurable, and peaceful life. Like the bull, they lay in the field, swatting the flies with their tail and left in solitude and peace.
.
They frequently suffer from illnesses of the neck, vocal cords, angina, tumors, diabetes, venereal disease, and diseases of the larynx, trachea, and thyroid.

Taurus in business – Taurus excels in natural sciences; banker, architect (with Libra and Capricorn), cook, jeweler, and agriculture. He or she may also be into botany, finances, trade management, accessory design, construction, and cosmetics.

Compatibility – Capricorn, Cancer, Virgo, Pisces

Celebrated Taurus – Adele, Queen Elizabeth, Dwayne "The Rock" Johnson, George Clooney, William Shakespeare, Mark Zuckerberg, Michelle Pfeiffer, Cate Blanchett, George Lucas, Cher, Jack Nicholson, Kenan Thompson, Gigi Hadid

Gemini (May 21-June 20) The Twins

Zodiac Quality – Mutable
Planet Ruler – Mercury
Zodiac Element – Air
Gems – Citrine, Moonstone, Pearl, White Sapphire

Gemini, the twins, is complex, elusive, contradictory, and dual-natured. It is the third sign of the Zodiac. Their ruler, Mercury, is the planet of youth. Those born under Gemini seem to exhibit the behavior and immaturity of youth. In their childlike demeanor, they can be gentle, adaptable, curious, quick learners, and affectionate.

Gemini love to speak to almost anyone, including strangers. They also love music, magazines, and books. They are great at adapting to social situations. Geminis enjoy travel as it gives them the ability to have new experiences and meet new people.

The negative side of Gemini is their craving to be the center of attention all the time. If the spotlight isn't on them, they'll leave. Relationships and friendships suffer because of this trait. Their desire feel important opens them to telling lies.

Physically, they frequently suffer from lung diseases, such as asthma and bronchitis.

Gemini in business - Publishing, literature, medicine (neuropathy, psychiatry, psychotherapy), technology, brokerage, painting, and journalism

Compatibility – Best with Aries, Libra, and Aquarius

Celebrated Gemini – Johnny Depp, Bob Dylan, Marilyn Monroe, Judy Garland, Paul McCartney, Chris Evans, Angelina Jolie, Prince, Venus Williams, Walt Whitman, Natalie Portman

Cancer (June 21-JULY 22) The Crab

Zodiac Quality – Cardinal
Planet Ruler – Moon
Zodiac Element – Water
Gems – Quartz, Crystal, Opal, Pearl

Cancer, the fourth sign of the Zodiac, is a water sign and ruled by the Moon. Those born under this sign are extremely intuitive and very sentimental. Of all the signs of the Zodiac, they are the hardest to get to know. They care greatly for their home and family and prefer to remain near to those they know.

People born under the sign of Cancer are tenacious, extremely imaginative, persuasive, sympathetic, and very loyal. They are hobbyists, and they appreciate the arts, low-key meals with good friends, and relaxing near the water.

Cancers can be moody (remember they are ruled by the Moon—the ebb and flow of emotions), pessimistic, insecure, and manipulative.

When they're not in a mood, the "crabs" have a good sense of humor, sometimes, even offbeat to some. They make good listeners and have a healthy sense of empathy for the troubles of others. Cancers make outstanding friends, are dependable, reliable, and most definitely loyal.

The pulmonary part of the body and stomach are ruled by Cancer. They are susceptible to mental problems and stomach illnesses.

Cancer in business - Nursing, politicians, interior decorators, horticulturists

Compatibility – Best with Virgo, Pisces, Scorpio, and Taurus

Celebrated Cancers – Meryl Streep, Robin Williams, Selena Gomez, Ariana Grande, Kevin Hart, Tom Hanks, Princess Diana, Tom Cruise, Giorgio Armani, Cyndi Lauper, Natalie Wood, Frances McDormand, Anjelica Huston

Leo (July 23-August 22) The Lion

Zodiac Quality – Fixed
Planet Ruler – The Sun
Zodiac Element – Fire
Gems – Ruby, Gold, Diamonds

Leo is the fifth sign of the Zodiac; it is a Fire sign ruled by the Sun. Leos are warm-hearted, humorous, creative, generous, and passionate. They are advocates of the arts and theater. They love having fun with their friends, camaraderie, and admiration from other people.

The lion is the realization of all the best traits of those born under this sign and is an apt symbol of this sign. Fire signs, such as Leo, draw people to them using their warm energy.

Leos are creative. They are the most dominant and spontaneous of all the signs in the Zodiac. Born leaders, they will either support or go against the status quo. Their personality is magnanimous, that gives them a great presence.

On the negative side of the sign, Leos can be extravagant, and their personality can border on arrogance. If they become domineering, they can smother their relationships with friends and significant others. Leos are family and community-oriented, and divorce can be especially disastrous and overwhelming for them.

Leos who are positive individuals are honest and decent people who will do the right thing regardless of the circumstance. They like to be organized, enjoy luxury, and are happy to share with others, so they can enjoy it as well.

Physically, Leos correspond to the heart, main arteries, spine, and back.

Leo in business - Actor, entertainer, announcer, advertising agent, artist, architect, business owner, comedian, DJ, event coordinator, hairstylist, financial planner, dancer, special education teacher, production artist, fashion designer

Compatibility – Best with Aries, Libra, Gemini, and Sagittarius

Celebrated Leos – Maya Rudolph, Helen Mirren, Jason Statham, Woody Harrelson, Robert De Niro, Jason Momoa, Robert Redford, Amy Adams, Madonna, Mila Kunis, Halle Berry, Chris Hemsworth

Virgo (August 23-September 22) The Maiden

Zodiac Quality – Mutable
Planet Ruler – Mercury
Zodiac Element – Earth
Gems – Carnelian, Moss Agate, Jade, Blue Sapphire

Virgo is the sixth sign of the Zodiac, ruled by Mercury. They are hardworking, practical, analytical, and loyal. They love animals and enjoy reading books, nature, and cleanliness.

They are always thinking, and they are detail-oriented and nurturing. They aren't opposed to being alone but enjoy the idea that someone is needing and appreciating them, even if that someone is far away. Virgos are earth signs, and they apply that element to working with pottery or woodworking.

Neither loud nor bossy, they are incredibly good at developing strategies that make life easier and share it with anyone who sees the value. Virgos sometimes go overboard with work, and they take on more than they should.

One negative aspect of Virgos is their extreme attentiveness to their health and everyone else's. They are opinionated and will share their opinions with others regardless of whether they've been asked for their opinion or not.

If they think that the people around them are not doing their job efficiently or living up to their potential, they judge them, which can be a bit off-putting.

On Virgo's positive side, they love to laugh. They are kind, patient, and truly compassionate. They can be strong, silent types and think creatively. They revere family.

Physically, Virgos suffer from their nervous system, insomnia, stomach problems, intestines, and pancreas.

Virgo in business - Veterinarian, lab technician, nutritionist, office manager, environmental journalist, life skills coach

Compatibility – Best with Taurus, Cancer, Capricorn, and Scorpio

Celebrated Virgos – Beyoncé, Keanu Reeves, Paul Walker, Adam Sandler, Freddie Mercury, Pink, Selma Hayek, Sophia Loren, Mother Teresa

Libra (September 23-October 22) The Scales

Zodiac Quality – Cardinal
Planet Ruler – Venus
Zodiac Element – Air
Gems – Diamonds, Blue Sapphire, Emerald, White Marble

Ruled by the planet Venus, Libra is the seventh sign of the Zodiac. Libra is about balance as the symbol for their sign indicates. Of all the signs of the Zodiac, balance is what Libra needs more than any other sign.

The balance between family life, work, social, and recreation is what Libra would like to have—some time in their life. Libras take time to make up their minds in order to arrive at the right decision, and can seem senseless to take so long to reach a decision.

They are the diplomats of the Zodiac, as they are cooperative, gracious, fair-minded, and social. When others are happy, they're happy, and they're the happiest when their world is balanced.

Libras can be charming, and they draw others to them. They meditate to help them find the balance that they need. A positive Libra is just and fair and becomes upset if a situation isn't that way.

The negative side of Libras is they take just about forever to make a decision, frustrating anyone who's waiting for them to make one. It may appear to others that they're absent-minded or even lazy. If a situation seems unjust or unfair to them, they will argue about the situation. Libras do not like confrontation in the form of family scenes or violence.

Libras are associated with the kidneys, urinary tract, and reproductive organs. They can also have sensitive blood vessels and skin. They frequently suffer from inflammation of the urogenital organs and diabetes.

Libra in business - Graphic designer, human resources, makeup artist, lawyer, set designers, musicians, photographers, models, actors, and public figures

Compatibility – Best with Leo, Sagittarius, Gemini, and Aquarius

Celebrated Libras - Mahatma Gandhi, John Lennon, Simon Cowell, Snoop Dog, Emilia Clarke, Gwen Stefani, Carrie Fisher, Kate Winslet, Serena Williams

Scorpio (October 23-November 21) The Scorpion

Zodiac Quality – Fixed
Planet Ruler – Mars, Pluto
Zodiac Element – Water
Gems – Aquamarine, Coral, Topaz, Obsidian, Beryl, Apache Tear

Scorpio is the Mars-ruled eighth sign of the zodiac. Scorpio's element is water, but, unlike Pisces and Cancer, the water is hot. Astrologers consider that the sign is more connected to Pluto, which recently lost its planet status.

Scorpio is a water sign that is passionate, stubborn, brave, resourceful, and someone who can be a true friend. Long-term friendships, the truth, and teasing those who they know will not take offense are things that this sign appreciates.

The scorpion that represents this sign isn't aggressive until someone aggravates and provokes them. Even after someone does irritate them, they would rather not fight but be contemplative about the situation. They are secret-keepers and intensely feel emotion more than any other sign. This gives Scorpio the ability to get to the bottom of any issue or situation and help people.

On the negative side, Scorpios have a desire to inflict revenge on someone. Scorpios do not forget those who have wronged them and often hold a grudge.

On the positive side, the self-control that Scorpios have in practically every other part of their lives is admirable. Because they are so self-controlled, they expect others to emulate them. They are disciplined, protective, and giving and expect to receive the same from others.

Scorpio in business - Financial advisor, physician, engineer, researcher, psychologist, pharmacist, marketing associate, market analyst, occupational therapist

Compatibility – Best with Pisces, Virgo, Cancer, and Capricorn

Celebrated Scorpios - Grace Kelly, Indira Gandhi, Scarlett Johansson, Jodie Foster, Leonardo DiCaprio, Bill Gates, Matthew McConaughey, Ryan Gosling, Pablo Picasso

Sagittarius (November 22-DECEMBer 21) The Archer

Zodiac Quality – Mutable
Planet Ruler – Jupiter
Zodiac Element – Fire
Gems – Ruby, Sapphire, Turquoise, Topaz, Amethyst

Those born under the fire sign of Sagittarius are ruled by Jupiter. Sagittarius is the ninth sign of the Zodiac. Sagittarians are creative, adventurous, and happy. They have a love for travel, meeting new people, and learning new things. They are idealistic and generous, and they have a good sense of humor.

Mundane or normal routines are not for this Fire sign. Without variety in their lives, they become restless. Their love of traveling and adapting to new experiences makes them a lot of fun. They have an abundance of friends.

On the negative side, a confined Sagittarius will bring out a rude and uncooperative fire sign. They rarely follow through with plans that border the grandiose because they are easily sidetracked.

On the positive side of Sagittarius, they are intelligent, and enjoy being around like-minded people. They are spiritually inclined and creative. Sagittarians will travel to places to seek enlightenment in all ways.

Sagittarius dominates the buttocks and thighs and can suffer from numerous and varied weaknesses, depending on the rest of the horoscope and its aspects.

Sagittarius in business - Uber driver, tourism specialist, freelance writer, environmental engineer, publisher, international travel consultant

Compatibility – Best with Aquarius, Leo, Aries.

Celebrated Sagittarians – Richard Pryor, Steven Spielberg, Miley Cyrus, Brad Pitt, Jay-Z, Zoë Kravitz, Kaley Cuoco, Jane Fonda, Bruce Lee, Winston Churchill, Jimi Hendrix, Ludwig van Beethoven

Capricorn (December 22-JANUARY 19) The Goat

Zodiac Quality – Cardinal
Planet Ruler – Saturn
Zodiac Element – Earth
Gems – Ruby, Agate, Garnet, Black Onyx

Saturn ruled Capricorn is the tenth sign of the Zodiac and an Earth sign. Capricorn's symbol of a goat is significant, as it represents this sign's aim to climb higher. Capricorn is successful, regardless of any odds they may face. They are extremely goal-oriented. They work hard in order to reach their goals. Capricorn is self-disciplined, with a penchant to be a teacher or scientist. They also make good managers.

Music, family, and anything made well and are of quality are enjoyed by Capricorns. They take their life and career seriously because they are on a mission to achieve their goals. They tend to be intolerant of people who do not show the same respect for their own lives.

On the negative side, their effort to achieve their goals may seem boring to others. Capricorn people sometimes give the impression that they lack emotion; they can be stingy and selfish. They will refuse to see a situation for what it is and that they may be wrong about it. If there is anything that a Capricorn dislikes immensely, it is being wrong.

On the positive side, they make solid, realistic, and logical decisions. They're good at being able to see the bottom line. They have a dry sense of humor that, at times, borders on sarcasm. They are also family-oriented. They are extremely intelligent and do very well with analysis and numbers.

The total skeletal system, knees, and bones are ruled by Capricorn.

Capricorn in business - CEO, business analyst, architect, creative director, financial planner, copywriter, intelligence analyst, human resources manager

Compatibility – Virgo, Scorpio, Pisces, and Taurus

Celebrated Capricorns – Betty White, Dolly Parton, LeBron James, Julia Louis-Dreyfus, Muhammad Ali, Michelle Obama, David Bowie, Mary J. Blige, Elvis Presley, Martin Luther King, Jr.

Aquarius (January 20-FEBruary 18) The Water Bearer

Zodiac Quality – Fixed
Planet Ruler – Uranus
Zodiac Element – Air
Gems – Amethyst, Garnet, Moss Agate, Opal, Magnet

Aquarius is ruled by Uranus and is the eleventh sign of the Zodiac. Some Aquarians take delight in saying they are ruled by Uranus because they consider themselves originals and eccentrics and associate themselves with other qualities we find distinctive in individuals.

Although the symbol for this sign is a water-carrier, Aquarius is an air sign and considered rational, social, and communicative individuals. They are very intellectual and friendly.

Aquarians may seem to be detached emotionally as a friend to others. However, when you get to know them better, you'll find they are more involved emotionally on a deeper level and make for a true friend. Individuals born under this sign tend to be comedic and will look to cheer people up when they are sad or are suffering from any issues.

Although Aquarians appreciate having significant relationships with others, they are extremely independent. They flourish in their freedom and thrive on the ability to come and go as they please. Aquarians, without their freedom, are like being deprived of oxygen. Trying to tie them down or restrict them will make them flee. This is not the most free-spirited sign in the Zodiac, yet they certainly enjoy having freedom more than most.

Aquarians can be incredibly stubborn. This personality trait does not bode well at times and can lead to relationship and career failures. Even if there is a multitude of documentation that proves them wrong, they will stick to doing things their own way.

Although they are stubborn and often rebuff the evidence that finds fault in their conclusions, they don't impose their ideas on others. Aquarians have great respect for other people's ideas and opinions, and they have the ability to understand the differences and views of others.

On the negative side, they can become resentful and depressed if they don't have enough time to be alone with themselves. Aquarians engage in self-rumination, habits, and activities that may seem to others as eccentric. They indulge themselves by working on their hobbies.

Aquarians' demeanor may seem standoffish, and it takes quite a bit to push them over the edge. They will hold in whatever it is that bothers them until they can no longer deal with the situation, at which point, they'll explode and lose control.

On the positive side of this sign, they are probably one of the friendliest of all other Zodiac signs. They do well networking with others and make friends wherever they go. Aquarians are at ease in speaking with other people they may have just met, and they make the other person feel like they've known each other for years.

They do need time to be alone, and they do well with yoga or meditation. Their quiet observations of other people and events may be a surprise when conversing about their viewpoints and opinions with others. They have, at times, a view that is slanted and that others may not have considered or thought about.

Aquarians tend to suffer from the nervous system, circulation, and heart disease.

Aquarius in business – Research scientist, inventors, electronics, social networking, pilot, professor of physics or astronomy, computer programmer

Compatibility – Libra, Gemini, Aries, and Sagittarius

Celebrated Aquarians – Sharon Tate, Farrah Fawcett, Abraham Lincoln, Oprah Winfrey, Bob Marley, Lisa Marie Presley, Christian Bale, Mariska Hargitay, Harry Styles, Yoko Ono, Paul Newman, James Dean, Dr. Dre, Chris Rock

Pisces (February 19-March 20) The Fish

Zodiac Quality – Mutable
Planet Ruler – Neptune, Jupiter
Zodiac Element – Water
Gems – Amethyst, Aquamarine, Bloodstone, Jade, Sapphire

Pisces, the twelfth sign of the Zodiac is ruled by Jupiter. Some astrologers believe that those born under this sign are affected by Neptune.

Pisceans are extremely popular with just about anyone because they are even-tempered and relaxed by nature. They are less threatening to others they associate with. Pisceans are empathetic, compassionate, caring, highly emotional, and faithful individuals. They also tend to be more involved and caring about other people's problems instead of dealing with their own.

Pisces individuals prefer to spend time alone and withdraw into other worlds of their creation. They can be who they want to be and do anything they want to do in these worlds. They have a deep appreciation for art, and they travel to exotic places.

The negative side of Pisces is, due to their emotional makeup, they absorb the emotions of others to the point of falling ill, and they are fearful of making any decisions. They don't want to disagree with others, so they avoid making any decisions at all.

Pisces can be absent-minded and need a nudge every now and again to complete projects and tasks they begin. Managerial positions are not ones Pisces do well in, although this can be affected by other aspects of their horoscope.

The positive side of Pisces shows them to have empathy for the problems of others and reach out to those who are in need. They care deeply and may not exhibit their feelings on the surface. Pisces are empathetic, musically inclined, and have a deep understanding of human weaknesses.

The feet are ruled by Pisces, and they may suffer from bone spurs and bruising of the feet. They also have respiratory and circulatory problems as well. Their psyche is very sensitive, so they withdraw and isolate themselves from others.

Pisces in business - Production editor, graphics designer, physical therapist, filmmaker, mental health technician, photographer, human resources coordinator

Compatibility – Cancer, Scorpio, Taurus and Capricorn

Celebrated Pisces – Michelangelo, Albert Einstein, Gloria Vanderbilt, Sophie Turner, Stephen Curry, Rihanna, Steve Jobs, Johnny Cash, Kurt Cobain, George Harrison, Daniel Craig

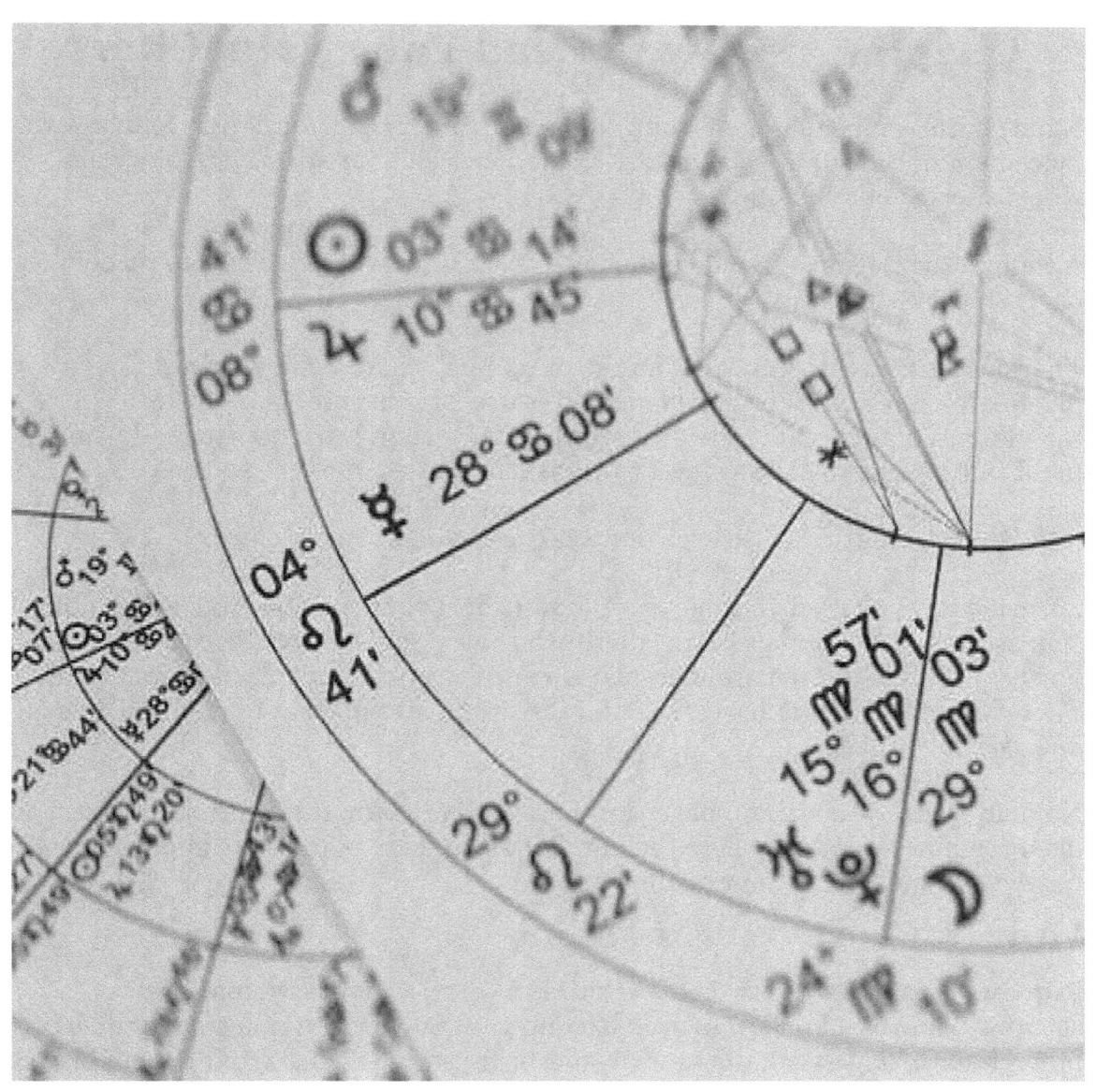

Your Natal Chart

Chapter 3: How to Read Your Natal Chart

Natal charts can be telling of who you are, the Sun sign of your birth, and how the placement of each of the planets are located in each house of the astrological wheel affects your overall persona.

Although some people find it confusing, this chapter will cover how to read your chart step-by-step.

Your natal chart, also known as an astrology birth chart, is the study of personality, the stars, and the planets. It is used to interpret and illustrate an individual's nature and predict their future. When you learn how to read your natal chart, you will have a view of yourself.

An astrology chart can disclose your weaknesses and your strengths.

So, every day you read your horoscope, you know your sun sign and compatible sign as well. If you've never had your birth chart done, it's not a bad idea to have one drawn for you. An astrologer may do one for a price, or you can get it online. There are sites that will have you enter the pertinent information and give you an analysis of your chart.

No matter how you want to have your natal chart drawn, the information that you need remains the same, where the Sun, Moon, and the planets are aligned in the universe at the time of your birth.

How to Find Your Sun Sign

Finding your sign – The Zodiac chart is a wheel and divided into twelve sections, known as houses. In order to find your Sun sign, you need your date of birth (month/day/year), the time of your birth, and the place. Your date of birth will fall into one of the sections. The section that your birthdate falls into is your Zodiac sign.

An example of this is January 28, 1947, 8:45 p.m. in New York, New York. This birthdate falls into the sign of Aquarius whose astrological sign dates are January 20-February 18. This determines the Sun sign.

The meaning of your Sun sign – The influence on your personality is influenced by your Zodiac sign. As an example, if you're born under the sign of Aquarius, you are a good friend, have a sense of humor, are extremely independent, and can be stubborn at times.

The information about the association of your personality traits with your Zodiac sign can be found in an astrology book that can be purchased online or at your local bookstore. You can also try your local library for books on astrology.

What affects how your Sun sign is read – The determination of your Zodiac sign is just one element of how your natal chart can be read. There are various aspects that influence the chart. The houses and planets need to be taken into consideration to get a full reading of your natal chart. That information is deemed from the date of your birth and the place where you were born.

The Astrological House – Do not confuse the Houses with the Zodiac wheel; they are not the same.

The Zodiac wheel rotates annually based on the yearly rotation of the Sun. The Houses represent the earth's rotation on its axis, which happens in a 24-HOUR rotation.

The natal planets (birth signs) in the birth chart are stationary, while the planets that rotate around the Sun (the Moon, Mercury, Saturn, Mars, Jupiter, and Venus and transcendental planets of Uranus, Neptune, and Pluto) consistently rotate in the Universe and move across the Houses.

Astrologers fuse the two systems when they draw a natal chart. It tells what a person's Sun sign is from the Zodiac, as well as identifies the person's personality traits.

To put it simply, a certain period of life will exemplify the essence of that House. We follow the sun's 365-day cycle and go through a solar cycle each year of all the Houses.

Your time of birth is crucial when your chart is being calculated. There is a shift every four minutes in the Houses, so even if individuals are born on the same day, their natal charts will be entirely different. This is based on whether they were born in the morning or the evening.

Houses in a natal chart reflect the different facets of an individual's life based on location and time of birth. They will interpret the obstacles or gifts you will face in life. Each planet, celestial point, or asteroid "lives" within a House. The placement of the planets gives you information about you, as well as how you synchronize with the world around you. As planets move in the Universe across these domains, distinctive embodied events, as well as emotional ones, are triggered. (Faragher, 2018)

So, an accurate time of birth can make all the difference in your natal chart. The chart will be inaccurate if your time is incorrect.

What the Houses Tell Us

Looking at your chart for the first time, it may seem to be a confusing compilation of symbols and lines across the face of the astrological wheel. Your focus is scattered, and it's not easy to know where you need to look first. Some areas have a number of symbols, some grouped together, while other areas have no symbols at all. Why is a portion of the natal chart blank? What are these symbols, and what do they mean? (Faragher, 2018)

Being able to read a natal chart is pretty uncomplicated. You just have to know where you need to begin. In order to begin, you need to locate the anchor of the chart, the Ascendant. The Ascendant in a chart is also known as the rising sign and is located at the furthest left point of the center horizon line. This discloses the zodiac sign that was materializing from the eastern horizon at the exact time of your birth. (Faragher, 2018)

The Sun brings to light our truth. The Moon is our emotional makeup, and the Ascendant exposes our landscape. Examples of the kind of landscape we're dealing with are one of independence and nonconformity that defines an Aquarius Ascendant, and security, stability, and loyalty will define a Taurus Ascendant.

The ruling planet of the natal chart is revealed by the Ascendant. Someone with an Aquarius Ascendant is ruled by the precise Saturn, while a Taurus Ascendant is ruled by the romantic Venus.

Locating the Ascendant

The Ascendant needs to learn how the houses will be labeled in the natal chart.

The Zodiac wheel can be looked at as a clock. You read this clock counterclockwise. Your Ascendant is located at the horizontal line that cuts across the "clock," so you will find your Ascendant at the 9 o'clock position. This position indicates the cusp of the First House.

The Astrological Houses Defined

The first six houses indicated the different facets of your life.

First House - The First House reflects you at the time of your birth, your physical appearance, temperament, attitude, and other qualities that are inherent in your makeup. Your personality is tremendously influenced by the sign and planets that are found in the First House.

Second House – This house is where your self-worth, money, personal assets, and your attitude toward these aspects in your chart are represented. How secure you will be financially and your well-being emotionally over the course of your life can be gauged by what planet and sign are found in this house. (wikiHow Staff, 2019)

Third House – Communication and transportation are represented by the Third House. The physical forms of communication, like email, text, or letters, are under this house. Also, traveling short distances and how others communicate with you are included. This also indicates how you learn, manner of speech, self-expression, and your mental attitude.

Fourth House – Family, home, property, your childhood, and internal emotions that correlate with these areas are represented in the Fourth House.

Fifth House – How you connect with children and relate to them are aspects of the Fifth House. Love affairs and romance are also part of the Fifth House. It shows how you have fun and approach things that bring you pleasure.

Sixth House – Your physical health and well-being through your life is represented in the Sixth House.

Along with the first six houses, there are six additional houses to round up all the information you can derive from your natal chart.

Seventh House – Committed, serious relationships are represented in the Seventh House. Romantic partnerships and marriage are ruled by this house. It can tell you what you need to have a long-term partner in the romance department.

Eighth House – This is the house of rebirth and transformation. Sex, birth, death, injuries, surgeries, decay, and healing are represented in this house.

Ninth House – This house represents travel that is long distance. The journeys found in the Ninth House are both metaphorical and physical. Journeys of over 500 miles, transformations, and emotional journeys are in the Ninth House.

Tenth House – Your career, status, aspirations, and ambitions are found in the Tenth House. Your place in a community is revealed in this house.

Eleventh House – The Eleventh House represents if and when your dreams will come true and is known as the house of hopes.

12TH House – This is the house of secrets, hidden emotions, and secret aspects of a person's past; all things that are hidden are exposed in the 12TH House. (wikiHow Staff, 2019)

How the Planets Play a Part in the Natal Chart

Finding the planets – The planets are found throughout the chart with different symbols representing them. Your reading is affected by the planets that pass through the different houses of your chart.

The First Set of Planets Are *Personal Planets*

The **Personal planets** are the planets whose orbits are closest to that of the Earth, and therefore closest to our physical being.

Sun – The Sun is indicated by a circle with a dot in the center of the chart. It is a personal planet that represents a person's purpose and identity.

Moon - A half-crescent moon shape reflects on the events that a person experiences in their life and how they react.

Venus – Venus is the symbol for women. It's a personal planet and represents what you are comfortable with and what you enjoy.

Mars - Mars is the male symbol. The planet represents your actions and will.

Mercury - Mercury is the symbol of the female but with two small lines at the top of the circle. The planet represents your capacity to perceive and relate to objects and individuals.

The Second Set of Planets Are Outer Planets

The **outer planets** move very slowly through the signs of the Zodiac. Sometimes it takes up to 15 years to complete a transit.

Jupiter – The symbol resembles the number 4 and represents how you assimilate with society and your personal growth

Saturn–This planet is represented by a symbol that resembles the number 5. It also represents the rules you create for yourself over your life, as well as your personal responsibilities

Uranus, Pluto, and Neptune each have symbols that are relatively complex, representing them.

Uranus – The symbol resembles the female symbol turned upside down. Your ability to learn and grow is represented by this planet.

Neptune – The symbol is an upside-down cross with two lines on each side and loops up. This planet indicates to your imagination and ideas.

Pluto – The symbol for this planet is a combination of Uranus and Neptune: a female symbol, facing upward and two lines on each side that loop up. Pluto is your capability for inner growth and change, denoting a deep and personal type of change.

Understanding and Interpreting Your Chart

To read your natal chart precisely, you need to consider where the planets appear. Where does the planet appear? In what house? Under which sign? Once you address these questions and acquire the information, you will get insight into your life path and personality.

The *Planets* describe what you enjoy and what it is that drives you. The *Houses* illustrate how and your manner of completing a given task. The *Signs* display in what areas you can foresee certain aspects of change or growth in your life. (wikiHow Staff, 2019)

If you are not experienced in drawing an astrologic chart, there are websites that will generate one for your use. All sites are not accurate, so take care in choosing the site you want to use. Read reviews and feedback from other users to get an idea as to how good the site is. It's possible to find a professional astrologer in your area who can create a chart for you.

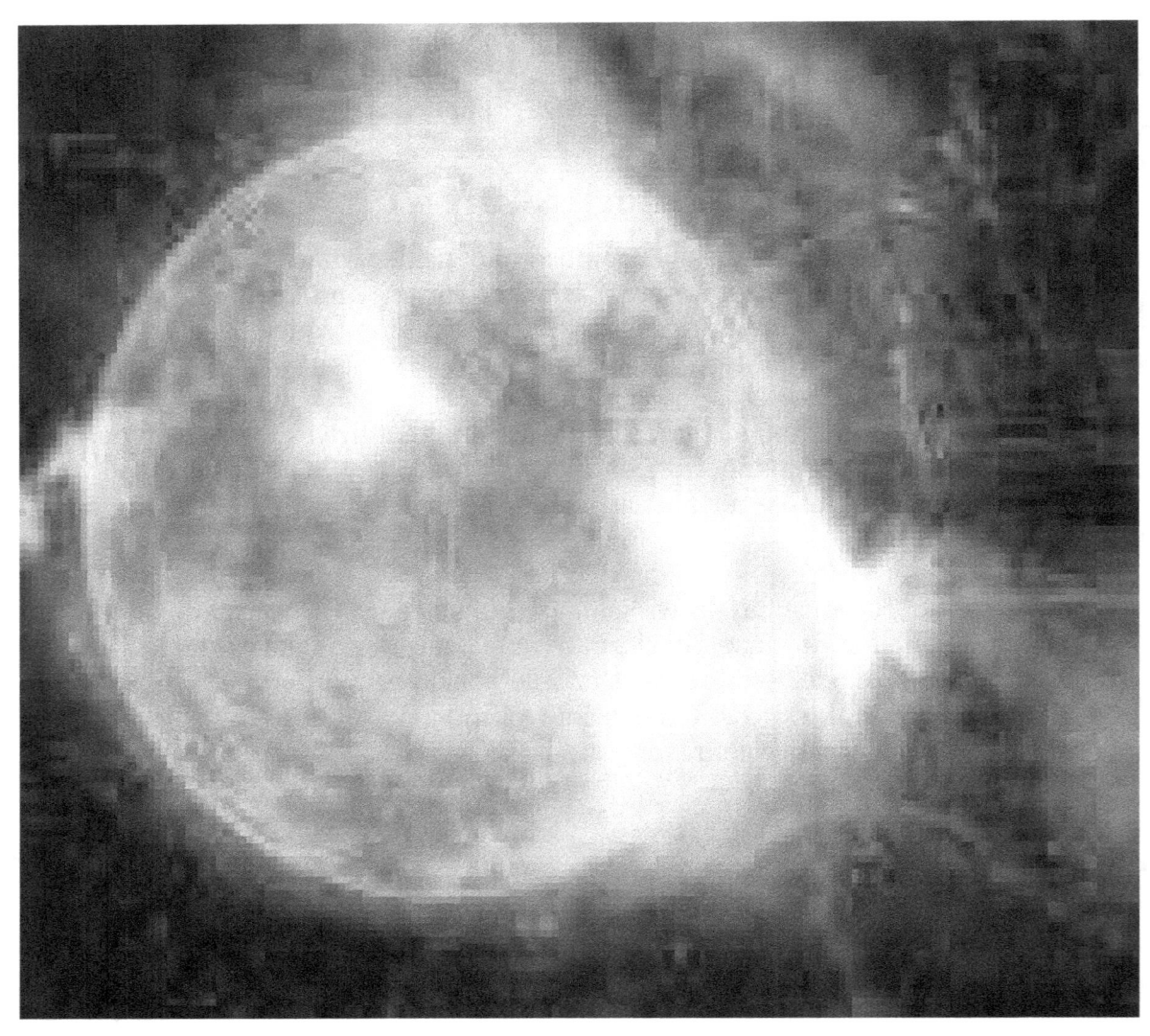

Your Sun Sign and You

Chapter 4: Your Sun Sign and You

Now that you know how your astrological chart is mapped using the Planets, Houses, and your Zodiac sign, let's concentrate on your Sun sign, the Zodiac sign you were born under.

As you've read in the previous chapters, your Sun sign is what dictates your zodiac personality. Your Sun sign is easily determined by the month, day of your birth, and the position of the Sun. For instance, a person's sun sign would be Taurus if the constellation Taurus was behind the Sun at the time of their birth. (Napier, Beth, 1995)

Know that the Sun sign in Astrology is the beginning; the tip of the iceberg. The study can take you into the mysteries that are deep within the universe. Yet, it all begins with the Sun, and that is what this chapter will cover.

These astrological outlines for each sign of the Zodiac are a general overview of each sign. Each of us has different aspects that were in play at the time of our birth, so the influence of other planets will tell other parts of your Astrological Chart.

Sun Signs in Astrology and Their Meaning

The sun sign is what describes your nature and personality traits. These traits remain constant throughout all the phases of life. Regardless of what happens, it is the image that all you get to know and see. It comes from the deepest, truest part of you. At the center of the Solar System is the Sun, which is actually a star. Like the sun, your sun sign illustrates the personal center that is uniquely you.

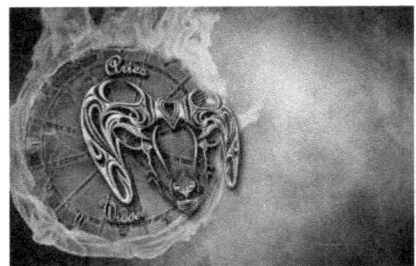

Aries (March 21-April 20)
The Ram

Aries is ruled by Mars, the first sign of the Zodiac and is a Fire sign. The best words to describe an Aries are confident, determined, optimistic, and passionate. They also exhibit a good amount of courage when needed.

Aries do well in managerial and leadership roles and enjoy physical challenges and individual sports. They also can display impatience and impulsiveness. They can also be short-tempered. If they don't use their talents, the possibility not to find their path in any role or job is unfortunately real.

March 21st is the spring equinox, the beginning of the new zodiac year, and new beginnings. This is what Aries represents. The Ram is impulsive, ambitious, energetic, and adventurous.

They have the ability to create new ideas that they put into action immediately. They are intelligent and are not afraid to take on new challenges head-on. They may become agitated if the ideas they implement do not show immediate results.

Aries is compatible with Aquarius, Leo, Sagittarius, and Gemini.

Taurus (April 21-May 20)
The Bull

The second sign of the Zodiac, Taurus, falls under the element of the Earth and is ruled by Venus. Those born under the sign of Taurus are devoted, stable, practical, reliable, and responsible. This is a very steady sign and is patient as well.

Although the bull is the symbol of this sign, people may be under the impression that Taurus is aggressive. Contrary to this belief, Taurus is peaceful and methodical. Their actions are deliberate, yet they are relaxed.

Taurus enjoys the sensual things of life, including food, luxury, and sex; everything that is luxurious is welcomed by this sign. Their luxury is the result of hard work. They enjoy cooking, music, quality in their surroundings, and gardening. Complications in their life or work environment, sudden change, and insecurity are things that Taurus does not welcome.

Well-balanced and stable, Taurus obeys the law, loves peace, and works to maintain their luxury. They have a strong aversion of being in serious debt, and they do everything they can to maintain their sense of security.

Taurus is astute and more practical than intellectual. They are known to formulate an opinion, and once it's established, it will remain unchanged, even if it's against the tide of popular consensus. Holding on to their ideals makes Taurus steadfast and true to their beliefs. They can keep cool during difficult times.

Their downside is their stubbornness and unchanging ideals that they adopt. This can make them challenging to get along with. Although they value the law and adhere to it, they may sabotage an authority figure if they feel their leadership is lacking.

On a positive note, this sign finishes what they begin. Leaving a project or task undone is rare. They make decisions that are usually the right ones due to their practice of deliberate thinking. Taurus enjoys spending time with loved ones and is family-oriented. Taurus is compatible with Capricorn, Cancer, Pisces, and Virgo.

Gemini (May 21-June 29)
The Twins

This twin sign is complex, contradictory, elusive, and dual-natured. Gemini is the third sign of the Zodiac; its element is Air, and it is ruled by Mercury.

Those who are born under this sign have a tendency to display the faults and behavior of the young as Mercury is the planet of youth.

Gemini has a childlike quality to them, making them curious, affectionate, and gentle. It also has them acting indecisive, nervous, and inconsistent. A Gemini loves speaking with everyone and anyone, total strangers included. They also appreciate books, magazines, and music.

Geminis are happy in groups, sharing concepts and ideas, having purposeful conversations, or going out to have fun. They rarely do anything alone. Social situations are their forte, and their love of talking with people makes their time socializing all the more pleasurable for them.

This sign is adventurous and carefree and enjoys traveling. It gives Gemini new opportunities to meet new people and acquire new knowledge.

Gemini's love to be excited intellectually, and they delve into the spiritual, mental, and physical arenas enthusiastically. Their personalities can be described as airy and breezy, which draws people to them. They love new experiences and will, at times, have them alone, though being alone is not the norm for this sign.

Gemini's negative side is that they must be at the center of attention at all times. If they aren't, and the attention is being paid elsewhere, they will leave the event, friendship, relationship, career, or party; you get the idea. Feeling important is a strong need for Geminis.

This sign tends to tell little white lies. Gemini will be rude and lack empathy when they focus only on themselves.

The positive side of Gemini is that they are charming, great conversationalists, and are interesting to be around. They are optimists and very funny. They hate to be bored, so they make their own enjoyment and fun to avoid the humdrum. Gemini is compatible with Leo, Libra, Aries, and Aquarius.

Cancer (June 21-JULY22)
The Crab

The Moon rules the water sign of Cancer, the fourth sign of the Zodiac. They are sentimental, sensitive, and emotional, and they care immensely for their home and family. They are profoundly intuitive and prefer to be near those who they know.

Tenacious, persuasive, sympathetic, and loyal, Cancers also have a great imagination. Hobbies are their favorite, and they enjoy doing them at home. They have an appreciation for art, and they love relaxing near water and getting together with good friends for quiet dinners and social events.

Cancers can be pessimistic, moody insecure, and manipulative.

The symbol for Cancer, the crab, personifies this sign because the crab's shell is carried on its back. Cancers are loyal to family and friends and remain close to home and are all about what revolves in their home. Their friends and family are their circles, and they tend to be dedicated to them. When a Cancer finds something that makes them happy, they will grab onto it.

Cancers like to be needed and feel secure in someone's love and caring. The best qualities of this sign are protective instincts and bravery. They do become moody and reclusive if their needs aren't met. They have a nurturing streak and are quite gentle with family and friends.

The negative side of Cancer is the tendency to be insecure, clinging to things and people. They can be moody, too, especially if they think a relationship is being lost. They will lie, although rarely. The lies are their feeling of insecurity about being alone.

Cancer is compatible with Taurus, Virgo, Pisces, and Scorpio.

Leo (July 23-AUGUST 22)
The Lion

Leo is ruled by the Sun; it is the fifth sign of the Zodiac and is a fire sign. Those born under this sign are generous, humorous, creative, and passionate. They get enjoyment from holidays, theater, fun with friends, and the admiration of others, and they love bright colors.

The lion is a fitting symbol for this sign because the lion is the epitome of the regal. Leos are warm individuals, and they use that energy to attract people, who people can't help but gravitate to them. People who are close to them feel loved and appreciated.

Leo, like the lion who is the king of the jungle, is the most creative, spontaneous, and dominant sign of the entire Zodiac. Positive, self-confident, and strong-willed, they are born leaders who can either support or revolt against any circumstances or a state of affairs.

Their charitable and selfless personality affords them a presence that is commanding. They get a tremendous amount of loyalty from those who work with them and are rather uncomplicated individuals.

The negative side of Leo has their arrogance on display if their sense of self-worth becomes greater than what it really is. They need to express themselves in a domineering manner, smothering their friends and significant others, but they need to be in charge is one of their faults. Those who don't understand a Leo may decide to leave. Family is very important to them, and divorce or loss of relationships or community can be very devastating and overwhelming to them.

The positive Leo is honest and decent and will do the right thing regardless of the circumstance. They excel in organizing, and they enjoy luxury. They also like the people whom they love and who are closest to them to enjoy the luxury as well. They are open to everyone, at least when they first meet them, and develop relationships. Some of these relationships become lifelong associations.

Leos are compatible with Libra, Sagittarius, Aries, and Gemini.

Virgo (August 23-September 22)
The Maiden

The Earth sign, Virgo, is ruled by Mercury and is the sixth sign of the Zodiac. Loyal, practical, kind, analytical, and hardworking, Virgo likes to connect with animals, enjoy nature, books, and everything that is clean!

Virgos are calm and collected, which is why the maiden was chosen to represent Virgo. On the surface, like a maiden, they appear to be calm and mild-mannered. However, there is a myriad of activity that is ongoing. They're always on the go; they never stop thinking and are always analyzing and assessing their situations.

They are extremely detail-oriented.

Virgos are nurturing individuals and don't mind spending time alone, as long as they are aware that someone appreciates and needs them. Virgos are not loud or overbearing and enjoy strategizing.

Virgo's negative side has them being too attentive to the health of others, as well as their own; they can be somewhat obsessive about it. They can be judgmental and opinionated and will share their opinions regardless if they're asked or not.

On the positive side, Virgos are extremely compassionate when it comes to others, patient, and kind, and they always enjoy a good laugh. They're creative thinkers and can sometimes be strong, silent types. Family is always important to them.

Virgo is compatible with Capricorn, Taurus, Cancer, and Scorpio.

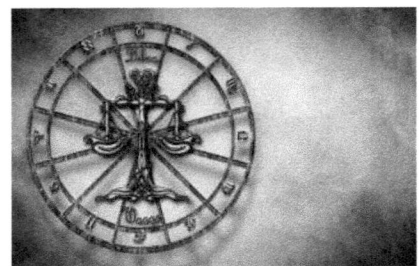

Libra (September 23-October 22)
The Scales

Libra is the seventh sign of the Zodiac, an Air sign represented by the symbol of the scales and ruled by Venus. This sign is about balance. They are the world's diplomats; they are cooperative, social, and fair-minded. They will always try to negotiate peace, whether between two people or two countries; this is an integral part of their nature.

Libras can give the impression of being unaware of the passage of time because it takes them quite a bit of time to come to a decision. Whether it's about what their company should do to improve service to a client or deciding on what luncheon sandwich they should order, they take their time to decide. The reason is that they need time to come to a decision that is the right one. However, when they do, it's almost always a good one, where everyone is happy in the end.

This sign likes harmony, sharing, and outdoors. They are gentle by nature. When others are happy, they're happy. When everything around them is balanced and harmonious, that's when they're the happiest.

Libras are very charming, and people are drawn to them. Any form of meditation for Libras is enjoyable because the balance that they seek is usually found in the moments of quiet and deep thought.

Libra's negative side is taking a long time to come to a decision, giving the appearance of absentmindedness or laziness. They also don't like the role of a manager or being in charge, yet they will make a point to be heard if necessary. They will argue a point if they feel a situation is unjust or unfair.

Libra is compatible with Leo, Sagittarius, Aquarius, and Gemini.

Scorpio (October 23-November 21)
The Scorpion

Scorpio, a water sign ruled by Pluto, is the eighth sign of the Zodiac. They are passionate, brave, and stubborn. They appreciate long-term friendships and are true friends.

The scorpion symbol illustrates the Scorpio persona well. This sign is not an aggressive one but will become irritated when they are prodded and aggravated. Although that provocation may move others to act, Scorpios become contemplative instead of drawn to fighting.

They are good at keeping secrets, and their emotions are felt by them more profoundly than any other sign. Scorpios' deeply felt emotions enable them to assist others with their problems. They also get to the core of any situation.

Scorpios' negative side is one you don't want to be on. The word "vendetta" is a word that some astrologers half-jokingly say Scorpio invented. Crossing them is one thing you really don't want to intentionally do because they never forget. In other words, don't get in their crosshairs.

They can also be suspicious, stubborn, and paranoid for no reason when they feel there are threats that don't really exist.

Scorpios' positive side is having enormous self-control in practically every part of their life. They are disciplined and protective. They are givers who expect to receive in return.

Scorpio is compatible with Virgo, Cancer, Pisces, and Capricorn.

Sagittarius (November 22-December 21)
The Archer

Sagittarius is a fire sign, ruled by Jupiter, and the ninth sign of the Zodiac. This sign is adventurous, creative, and happy. Those born under this sign have a love of travel, learning, and discovery of new things. They love meeting new people.

Sagittarians are generous and idealistic, and they have a good sense of humor. They don't like mundane routines or being tied down to a normal, repetitive one. Variety is their spice of life, and they become restless if there isn't enough of that.

They love to travel and search for new experiences, making them fun to be around. They have a large group of friends and socialize quite often.

The negative side of Sagittarius makes them rude and uncooperative when confined or tied down. At times, they create elaborate plans but don't follow through because they get distracted and easily sidetracked.

On the positive side, they enjoy being around people who are equally intelligent as they are. Sagittarius is also spiritually inclined and creative.

Sagittarius are compatible with Aries, Leo, Libra, and Aquarius.

Capricorn (December 22-January 19)
The Goat

Capricorn, the Earth sign ruled by Saturn, is the 10th sign of the Zodiac. The mountain goat is the symbol for Capricorn and illustrates this sign's ambition to climb higher. They are successful and goal-oriented, and they work hard to achieve their goals. They are not short-sighted, but they look at the long-term.

Their self-discipline is admirable. Some of the greatest leaders, scientists, and teachers in the world are born under Capricorn. They enjoy music and family, and they are very traditional. They love to observe the holidays with all the trimmings.

Achievement is very important to them and is serious about working toward a goal. They are intolerant of people who do not do the same.

The negative side of Capricorn is their commitment to the minutia of details and the big picture which appears dull to others. They are always thinking, but they give the impression of being emotionless to others. They can be selfish and stingy, and they may withhold information that is valuable as a strategy for their eventual gain.

On the positive side, Capricorns can make realistic and logical decisions. They are good at seeing the bottom line, and this ability makes them an asset to any corporate position they may hold. Their humor swings between dry and sarcastic but not in a mean way. They are extremely intelligent and do well with analysis and numbers.

Capricorns are compatible with Taurus, Scorpio, Virgo, and Pisces.

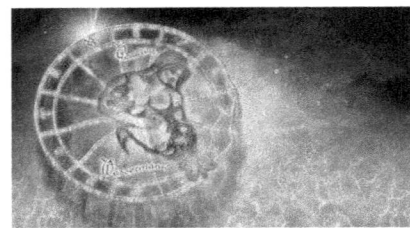

Aquarius (January 20-February 18)
The Water Bearer

Air sign Aquarius is the eleventh sign of the Zodiac and ruled and influenced by the outer planet of Uranus. Air signs are communicative, social, friendly, and intellectual, and they enjoy relationships. Their positive traits can be overshadowed by their penchant for being superficial.

Aquarians seem to be detached emotionally. However, when you get to really know them, you'll find they are on a much deeper plane when it comes to friendships and will find a true friend in them. If a friend or family member is feeling down, they'll be there to cheer you up.

Independence is an Aquarian's middle name and a large part of their persona. They enjoy deep relationships, but they value their independence. They love their freedom and like to have the ability to come and go whenever they want. Restricting them or tying them down will have them run in the other direction.

Aquarius can be extremely stubborn, which can occasionally interfere with their personal relationships and career. They may be shown a plethora of evidence that shows them they are wrong, but they will continue to insist on doing things their way.

However, in all their stubbornness, they do not impose their ideas on others. Aquarius has a unique quality in that they have respect for everyone's opinions and understand other people's different viewpoints and differences.

Not having their time alone is the negative side of Aquarius. They become resentful and even depressed when they don't get their space and alone time. They enjoy having time for their hobbies or extra-curricular activities which may seem bizarre to some.

The positive side of Aquarius is they are one of the friendliest of all the other signs of the Zodiac. They acquire friends easily, and co-workers often speak highly of working with them. They are great at networking and are at ease speaking with others as though they've known each other for years. This happens with people they've just met as well. Aquarius needs time for themselves, and they do well with meditating or practicing yoga.

Aquarius is compatible with Gemini, Sagittarius, Aries, and Libra.

Pisces (February 10-March 20)
The Fish

The 12TH sign of the Zodiac, Pisces is ruled by Jupiter, and its symbol is the fish. Pisces is compassionate, wise, intuitive, and artistic. They like sleeping, solitude, music, and spiritual themes. They are also romantic.

Criticism is not something they welcome, and they absolutely abhor cruelty to people and the animal kingdom. They also dislike people who come off as know-it-alls. They frequently dwell on things that happened in the past.

Pisceans are rather easy-going and are popular with almost any kind of crowd. Their nature tends to be submissive, making them less threatening to those whom they interact with.

This sign is selfless and helps others without any expectation of something in return. They are empathetic and emotional, faithful, caring, and compassionate. Sometimes, the troubles of others concern them more than their own.

Pisces withdraw from the real world and would rather spend time in the fantasy worlds of their making. In that world, they can be extremely wealthy. They travel the world and have a myriad of homes. They have a great appreciation for art, and they dream about traveling to exotic places.

The negative side of Pisces is how they take on the worry and problems of others. They worry themselves into illness. They don't do well in managerial positions but do excel as a support staff position.

The positive side of Pisces is their empathy for the troubles of others. They feel compassion for people who are not doing well in their lives. They are caring, and they feel deeply even if they do not show it on the surface.

Pisces is compatible with Cancer, Scorpio, Capricorn, and Taurus.

Moon Signs

Chapter 5: How to Determine Your Moon Sign

Your personality is dictated by your Sun sign, yet that is just one factor of what makes up who you are. Your emotions are part of our psychological makeup.

The Moon influences the second most significant factor of your natal chart after the Sun. It represents your emotions, moods, and how you react emotionally overall.

The Sun sign is determined by your month and day of birth. The Moon moves at a quick pace around the Zodiac, completing its full rotation in one month, visiting all the signs. It remains in each sign for approximately two days. The time of your birth comes into play to determine your Moon sign.

If the Moon is in the process of moving to the next sign on the day of your birth, knowing the time of your birth will help you get an accurate Moon sign placement. It would be ideal to have the exact time of birth, but an approximation of the time can help an astrologer establish which sign the Moon was in at the time of your birth.

The Moon causes the high and low tides of the oceans by the gravitational pull known as the tidal force. This force causes Earth and its water to create high and low tides. In comparison, our emotions have highs and lows, causing our emotions to be amplified and our behavior affected by the moon.

Probably since the beginning of time, the moon has been linked to the changes in our behavior and mood. Studies have found a link between the number of psychiatric emergencies and the cycle of the moon.

In ancient times, the full moon was a time of much socializing activity, while a new moon would leave us in darkness, where we would go inward and reflect, remaining at home.

Today, we don't use the full moon as our light to socialize and gather, yet the innate intuitiveness continues to be wired to follow the moon cycles. Being more sociable or a bit reclusive during the new moon may be the reason for your level of activity and mood changes.

The moon's energy intensifies and heightens our emotions. Like the changing tides, a full moon can bring up all your emotions, while a new moon will be a time of reflection and calm.

So let's look at how the sign and its ruling planet affect how the Moon's emotions affect you.

If your Moon is in each of these signs, this is what you can expect about your emotional makeup.

Moon in Aries

Mars is the strong-minded planet ruling Aries. The energy can either be assertive and motivated, or aggressive and determined. Mars can make you impulsive, intense, and quick to act and overreact at times. Your temper is fiery and short from this emotionally charged Moon and Mars combo.

Aries needs to be challenged and will go all out to find a specific level of excitement in any form. Although it is a good thing to release your bottled up energy, the person who is on the receiving end of that release may be left to feel wounded after you've moved on and forgotten about it.

Those born with the Moon in Aries have the ability, from an emotional point of view, not to hold any grudges. You are able to say what's on your mind, release it, forgive, and forget rather quickly.

Moon in Taurus

Venus, the love goddess and the beholder and lover of beauty, is the ruler of Taurus. This influences your inner mood. You are caring and sensitive and well-liked. However, your caring for others can make you a target to be taken advantage of.

In love, you are a giver and expect the same in return. You have a tendency to be controlling and possessive of your partner if you suspect they may be stepping out with another. You become hurt if you are disrespected or if your desires are not met.

You are open and loving if you are treated well. You can be the best friend or lover. Your surroundings affect you, and you do cope with life better if your surroundings are comfortable and secure.

Moon in Gemini

Gemini is ruled by the planet of communication, Mercury. If there isn't enough activity to give you mental stimulation, you will become bored easily. This leaves time to play tricks and be mischievous. You don't mean any harm; it's just for fun.

The challenge to a Moon in Gemini is slowing down and not to have an activity to constantly be a part of . You can stop and reflect on how you feel rather than how you *think* .

However, that is not so simple for a Gemini or a Gemini Moon. When your emotions are confronted, you would rather look at things how you want them to be, instead of how they really are.

You are curious, clever, and have a playfulness about you. You can be open-hearted and sentimental when you let your feelings show.

Moon in Cancer

The Moon rules Cancer, and the pairing with this sign makes you incredibly emotional and sensitive. With the quick change of signs the Moon makes, this consistent change can make you moodier than most.

You will rarely go against the way you feel, even if something appears to be reasonably sound. You will operate by your feelings and make decisions based on intuition and impulse.

Your feelings are hurt rather easily, but that outer shell of protection from your symbol, the crab, will have you protect yourself by pulling back and shutting down. You have emotional strength, that may appear fragile but is actually pretty resolute.

You give people an ample amount of warnings and chances, and if they continue to provoke you or tinker with your heart and emotions, you have been known to cut all ties without a backward glance. The door is locked once you decide to close the door. When treated well, you are a protective, nurturing, and loyal friend or partner.

Moon in Leo

The center of our solar system, the Sun, the most powerful of forces and ruler of Leo, gives you the ability to have the resilience and confidence to take charge of your emotions, as well as your life.

You endeavor on being a leader, and when your talents are admired and recognized, you excel. You do tend to be bossy when your emotions are out of sorts, along with your conceited and petty attitude.

You are generous of the spirit and heart, extravagant, and exuberant. You care deeply for those who give you love and support. Your pride and emotions are connected, and since you love being the center of attention, you have high emotions when you are in the front and center, proud of what you do and who you are.

Moon in Virgo

You are an intelligent being if your Moon is in the sign of Virgo, ruled by Mercury. You have a strong sense of self and are emotionally reserved.

Your tendency to get caught up in the minutia of details and over-analysis distracts you from how you feel emotionally and the big picture in general.

You have a tendency to be picky and critical. This is the way Virgos are but with only those people you care about and love. Anyone else wouldn't even be a blip on your caring radar. You will reach out and offer your care and advice to only those who appreciate the effort, which is when you are at your emotional best.

The person you are most critical of is yourself. You critique yourself the hardest because you strive for an outcome that is frequently unattainable. You need to be kind to yourself, which is the best solution to your criticizing yourself.

Moon in Libra

Libra is ruled by Venus, the planet of grace, beauty, and love. These are all the things a Libra must have. Libra is the sign of balance and the sign of the scales. Your emotions are balanced by keeping the people you interact with. You also keep your environment balanced. You like to keep it all as harmonious as possible.

You sometimes put the needs of others before yours and keep everything and everyone agreeable because you look to get along with people. That may be a good thing for other people, but your balance is upset and unsettled if you're in disagreement with others.

You may give up too much of your needs and go too far in the direction of pleasing others and feel you've been taken advantage of and become irritable.

Look for the balance between the needs of others and your needs—that is the balance you will need.

Moon and Scorpio

Pluto, the planet of transformation is Scorpio's ruler. Pluto influences the inner world of those with their Moon in Scorpio with power, intensity, and the desire to look deep for the truth. Honest connections with others include passionate, sensitive, and strong expression that brings emotional fulfillment.

When you are angry or upset, you'll never let on to others because you hide your emotions under a glacial demeanor that does not reveal your disposition. This is your secret weapon, and others may become suspicious.

You live for emotional intensity and the drama of life because it gives you the feeling of being alive. However, when you have a tight rein and control over your own emotions, you feel the most powerful.

You have an intense emotional commitment with those you care for, and you surround them with protectiveness and love that is incomparable by any other.

Moon in Sagittarius

Jupiter, the planet of expansion and wisdom, is the ruler of Sagittarius. Your emotions are high with the desire to explore the world of different beliefs. You have a thirst for knowledge, and you have the spirit of adventure.

You are a truth seeker and have a feeling of being unsettled if you are obliged to keep a secret rather than tell others quite bluntly what they need to know. You are of the mind that even if the truth hurts, it will allow you to feel satisfied and relieve the emotional tension.

Living life to the fullest is how you want to experience life and prefer that someone is beside you, enjoying it with you, even if a commitment is something you shy away from.

You are, by nature, optimistic and positive, and you won't remain in a negative mood for long. Your outlook on life is forward-looking, and that's how you like it.

Moon in Capricorn

The planet of reality and ruler of Capricorn, is serious Saturn. This is also the planet of the teacher and will infuse your mood with a driven, solitary, and no-nonsense quality.

In order to keep your emotions balanced, there is a time between the busy schedule you keep and getting together with others in the social world. You need time to decompress. But it is important not to remain in solitude for too long; you need time to avert a down-in-the-dumps blues.

You do well when mixing with others, but you can be at ease with your own company. You need to feel that you have a feeling of worth in this world. It is in your later years when you have a sense of achievement that you can feel settled and relaxed. Your heart is not something you give easily to another, but when you do find someone special to trust and love, you give them your all.

Moon in Aquarius

Uranus, the planet of innovation and independence, is the ruler of Aquarius. This planet infuses your mood with your refusal to walk in another's shoes and individuality that separates you from the rest.

A groundbreaker, you can be in your own world, giving the impression that you are standoffish when, in reality, you are categorizing things in your mind. People who are secure within their own selves do better in associating with someone whose Moon is in Aquarius.

If your Moon is in Aquarius, you need your freedom to be who you are, and you need to be with those who understand this about you and not take your "distancing" personally. Only then can your emotional balance be achieved; otherwise, you will have to deal with someone else's anxieties.

You and your emotions can be unpredictable. To soothe your soul and your emotions, having an extensive conversation with someone will do you well.

Moon in Pisces

Neptune, the planet of compassion and inspiration, is the ruler of Pisces and is the influence of your emotions with deep empathy and sensitivity. Meditative silence allows you to gain access to your imagination and dreams, make a spiritual connection, and keep your emotions controlled. What helps you to be effective in the world is a balance between reality and escapism—to have a place to claim as a sanctuary, an escape where you feel comfortable. Safety is a major factor in your happiness.

Those with their Moon in Pisces are highly sensitive and show the feelings of their emotional state. For this reason, and because there is an innocence about you, there is a need for you to be careful of the people you select and allow to share your life with. You have a tendency to take on other people's emotions and attitudes because you care too much.

The symbol of the two fishes is a sign of duality, and in order to maintain emotional stability in your life, you need to have a balance between your mind and your heart. You will feel at peace with yourself if you follow this guideline.

Your Sun Sign ↓	Your Hour of Birth											
	6am to 8am	8am to 10am	10am to 12pm	12pm to 2pm	2pm to 4pm	4pm to 6pm	6pm to 8pm	8pm to 10pm	10pm to 12am	12am to 2am	2am to 4am	4am to 6am
Aries ♈	♉	♊	♋	♌	♍	♎	♏	♐	♑	♒	♓	♈
Taurus ♉	♊	♋	♌	♍	♎	♏	♐	♑	♒	♓	♈	♉
Gemini ♊	♋	♌	♍	♎	♏	♐	♑	♒	♓	♈	♉	♊
Cancer ♋	♌	♍	♎	♏	♐	♑	♒	♓	♈	♉	♊	♋
Leo ♌	♍	♎	♏	♐	♑	♒	♓	♈	♉	♊	♋	♌
Virgo ♍	♎	♏	♐	♑	♒	♓	♈	♉	♊	♋	♌	♍
Libra ♎	♏	♐	♑	♒	♓	♈	♉	♊	♋	♌	♍	♎
Scorpio ♏	♐	♑	♒	♓	♈	♉	♊	♋	♌	♍	♎	♏
Sagittarius ♐	♑	♒	♓	♈	♉	♊	♋	♌	♍	♎	♏	♐
Capricorn ♑	♒	♓	♈	♉	♊	♋	♌	♍	♎	♏	♐	♑
Aquarius ♒	♓	♈	♉	♊	♋	♌	♍	♎	♏	♐	♑	♒
Pisces ♓	♈	♉	♊	♋	♌	♍	♎	♏	♐	♑	♒	♓

Your Rising Sign

Chapter 6: Your Rising Sign

The third element of your astrological chart that determines the development of a person's character, as well as how it influences their physical characteristics, is your Ascendant, also known as your Rising sign.

How others see you is what your Ascendant represents. In your first meeting with someone, you will most likely be meeting their rising sign. Those who know very little about astrology could be surprised how much influence their ascendant applies to their character.

The ascendant is a significant part of your natal chart and based on the sign and degree that was on the horizon right at the time of your birth. For example, if the sign of Leo was at the 9 o'clock position on the horizontal line of your astrological chart, it is your Ascendant.

The way to locate your ascendant to apply it to your natal chart is to have not only the date of your birth but also the time and place of your birth as well. Every two hours, the ascendant changes, which is a reason for you to try having the most accurate information possible about the time of your birth.

The rising sign has an importance of its own, separate from your Sun sign. The twelve astrological houses are set in their positions from the rising sign.

The only way for your Sun sign and Ascendant to be the same is if you were born at dawn. So, for example, if you were both Sun in Scorpio and Scorpio rising, it would be known as a double Scorpio.

Aries Ascendant

Aries ascendants are quick and direct. They usually do rather than think. They never plan ahead. They simply begin doing whatever it is without much forethought and get it done.

A person with an Aries ascendant is not aggressive, as much as they are candid in what they say. Their manner is direct and youthful, and when they see what they want, they usually go after it. However, there's no intent of malice in their actions.

There are some Aries rising individuals who are competitive, but the pressure is usually on themselves. They strive to come out on top in all things they do. They are quick in every action they take—walking, getting dressed—and they have little time or patience in dawdling.

They're quick in the temper department as well, but that is quick to disappear and move on as well. Aries rising people rarely hold grudges.

People with Aries rising sign love action and lots of activity. Sometimes, completing things that they had begun doesn't come easily.

Aries Ascendants have a quick walk with their head leaning slightly forward, like the ram. They complain of sinus irritation, eye problems, and headaches. Acne and rashes on their faces and upper body are also maladies they may have.

Aries rising people are self-reliant, and this is generally learned from their early childhood experiences. They are usually willing to compromise in relationships, and they are very close to those whom they care for.

Taurus Ascendant

Taurus rising is slow, capable, and steady. This is how to describe those born with a Taurus Ascendant. Their stamina and fortitude are tremendous. They are very loyal to the people they care about. They radiate stability and exhibit personal presence yet, generally, do not come on strong.

Generally, the sign on the Ascendant discloses how people begin new things. By nature, Taurus usually resists change, and it can be a bit difficult to persuade those with Taurus rising sign since this sign is frequently fixed in their ways. They usually respond by feeling things out before they act. Their security is their most important considerations before they decide to engage in anything new.

These Taurus rising natives are careful and cautious and are not known for being flexible, considering the fixed sign on the ascendant. They are single-minded in their thinking.

Taurus rising sign enjoys the luxury and good things in life. Their weakness can be self-indulgence, and they place quite a bit of value on their material items.

Taurus rising individuals have physiques that are solid and strong. They rarely dress flashy or showy, and they usually like quality clothing and dress for comfort.

These Taurus rising natives don't break up their relationships easily and are somewhat possessive in their partnerships. They don't display jealously yet view their partners as personal property. They consider loyalty to be extremely important.

Taurus rising individuals are very sensual and prefer the stability of one-on-one partnerships, and although they enjoy calm and harmony, their partnerships may be passionate.

These Taurus rising natives have stability about them that is soothing and inner peace that is comforting to be around.

Gemini Ascendant

People born with Gemini rising sign look at the world as a place to learn. They are interested and curious about those around them. They love to freely move around, ask questions, and mingle with others.

They have a restless streak and are quick in their physical expression. Gemini rising sign gives off an air of impatience even if it's not meant. There is wittiness to Gemini Ascendants that sometimes can intimidate those who are of a more sensitive nature.

People with Gemini rising sign has an aptitude with words, which can be a great asset. However, these individuals identify a bit too much with their cleverness. They forget their personal communications with others to nurture and cultivate those around them. Although a lack of warmth in the way they present themselves is generally a façade, it is not immediately clear to most that a Gemini is hiding behind a mask.

There are two descriptions of the presentation that is common with Gemini Ascendants. One is changeable, talkative, and a bit quirky. They are fun and interesting. They explain and clarify things, whether it's an opinion, the world, or even their own behavior.

The other description is an intellectual with a cool attitude and who is clever and witty but not as changeable and animated or cheerful as the other group. They have sharp views, and their manner can be abrupt.

Regardless of which style they are, Gemini rising individuals are analytical. Their observations are progressive, and they are mentally active. At times, they are easily sidetracked because they have a large capacity of curiosity. Their minds are quick, while their attention span can be short.

Gemini rising individuals frequently look for a particular amount of space and freedom for their personal self. Intellectual debates and the exchange of ideas and ideals are enjoyed by these Gemini Ascendants.

A Gemini always welcomes some freedom and is willing to give breathing room and space to their partners.

Cancer Ascendant

Cancer rising people give the appearance of being gentle. When they enter a room, they don't burst into it. Instead, they move to the sides of the room and work their way to the center. They get flustered, particularly in public, and are sensitive to their environment.

When they are on an unfamiliar ground or feel threatened, their first instinct is to be self-protective, withdrawing shyly when new situations arise. On the whole, Cancer rising people appear to be caring, sweet, and even innocent. They seem unassuming enough to be approachable. However, there are those Cancer Ascendants who have withdrawn so much to become not as approachable as it might seem.

Cancer rising people look for security and structure in a relationship and partner. These individuals are at their best when they have a partner who exhibits financial and emotional stability, strength, and capability.

Many Cancer Ascendants like it when there are defined rules and structure in their relationship. Their security is a need that Cancer ascendants have and will give up some of their personal freedom in order to have that security.

Cancer rising people appear to be quiet and family-oriented, but they have a pragmatic approach to marriage.

Leo Ascendant

Leo rising people get noticed without trying. They radiate a magnetism and energy that draw the attention of others. Sometimes, it's because they can be loud, giving attention to their appearance. At other times, it's their regal manner that gets the attention and interest from others.

Leo Ascendants are self-aware of themselves, including their physical appearance. They consider how others appear, and they are aware of the people they are with, the surroundings they are in, and what it does to their own image. Leo rising people think they're on a stage, even in their own homes.

They have a natural optimism and enthusiasm about beginning anything new, and sometimes, they overestimate things, including themselves. Leo rising people are good promoters, and they can be walking commercials.

Leo Ascendants pay attention to their mannerisms and appearance and have a strong physical structure. They usually like hairstyles and clothing that are youthful, while their manner is strong and autocratic.

Regardless of their age, people with Leo rising sign are generous and spirited, warm, and love to have fun. They basically are kids at heart.

Leo rising individuals, and how selfless they are, will be altered by which sign and house the Sun is at the time of their birth. This is because the Sun is the ruler of a Leo Ascendant. Regardless of the placement of the Sun, Leo rising people are optimistic and self-aware. They always want to create a stir when they can.

Virgo Ascendant

Virgo rising natives frequently downplay their appearance and mannerisms, although it depends on where Mercury, Virgo's ruling planet, was positioned in the astrological chart at the time of their birth.

Virgo rising people have reserved aura and intelligence that is distinct. Actually, they are a bit shy and need time before they can warm up to people and situations to analyze them. Their analytical nature can be accepted for what it is, or it can be seen as cool, critical, and, in a manner, standoffish.

Body awareness is Virgo rising sign's biggest personality attribute. Virgo ascendants are conscious of any signals of discomfort that their body gives them. They are particularly concerned with their physical health, and some Virgo rising natives are interested in mind-body awareness and engage in exercises like yoga.

Although they have good appetites, Virgo ascendants are picky about their food and what they ingest into their bodies.

These Virgo rising natives tend to worry, particularly when encountering new situations. There are details that others overlook that a Virgo rising will notice down to the tiniest one.

Virgo rising natives attract or are attracted to people in need. Because of this, their relationships may be complex. Virgo's tendency is to appear professional and coolly possessed, yet their relationships can become disorderly and muddled because these natives do not see clearly when it comes to their partnerships and partners.

Virgo rising natives possess a quiet charm. Once given the opportunity to warm up to new situations and people, one can discover that they have quite a bit to offer. They'll be helpful to you when there's a problem or issue; they will stick their neck out for you, and you'll be amazed at their modesty hidden under that aloof and critical manner.

Libra Ascendant

Libra Ascendants appears to be liked by everyone. They present themselves as pleasant, nice, and fair, but if you look a bit closer, they seem to have a few problems in their relationships.

These Libra rising natives attract others to them without even trying, and some have a string of relationships. They just don't know what to do without having a significant other.

Libra rising have a gentle approach with everyone, a charming smile, an even-tempered image, and they generally appear to be able to smooth everything over. Most of these Libra Ascendants pay quite a bit of attention to their personal appearance—what they wear, the color, the way they walk, and their hair. Even if they were not blessed with good looks, they're attractive to others.

Libra rising natives usually use a soft sell approach when trying to win others over (which is usually all the time), and they can be extremely, extremely persuasive. Their worst quality is maintaining their nice person image by passing the responsibility in a situation or issue on to someone else. However, they do make good mediators and will be the first to help you.

Libra rising natives are attracted to active, competent partners. Their relationships often have competitiveness or bickering in the mix until they realize they have to drop the nice person image every now and again, and they need to end the "blaming their partner game" for everything that goes wrong.

Scorpio Ascendant

Scorpio rising has quite a bit of presence. There is an aura about them that gives notice to the world that they won't be pushed around. Their demeanor commands respect and fear, in some cases. Quiet or loud, Scorpio rising people always seem to be determined and powerful.

Whether you love or hate Scorpio rising natives, they very rarely go through life unnoticed. When faced with the idea they get strong reactions from others, they are somewhat bewildered.

Their ability to see right through people and their façade can be intriguing to some and intimidating to others. When Scorpio rising people deal with others, they usually look for answers by reading between the lines. They get rid of surface details when they get a feel for the situations and people around them.

Scorpio rising natives need to control their environment and value their privacy to the point that borders on paranoia. They plan their moves rather deliberately and rely on their capability to examine situations and others.

Scorpio rising people are attracted to natural, commonsensical partners. They value reliability in their partners and, in general, don't waste their time on flighty partners. They look for partners that can give them a complete commitment.

Sagittarius Ascendant

This rising sign represents new things to encounter, a world filled with adventure and hope. Enthusiasm and faith are unmistakable with Sagittarius rising people. The enjoyment of exploring, big promises, and grand schemes are its themes. However, a not-so-strong characteristic of Sagittarius is follow-through.

Restless and frequently active, Sagittarius rising natives always seem to be seeking something that's just out of reach. Many do this over their lifetime. They can be direct at times to a fault but are appealing enough to be forgiven. They have lots to offer, and their observations and opinions are usually interesting, although they sometimes don't provide enough details.

Sagittarius rising people like to tell others exactly what they are, and they have opinions about everything. Some people in this position have a way of radiating a certain level of confidence, and some may even call them overly optimistic or even naïve. Even the quiet Sagittarians don't shy away from experience and life.

Sagittarius rising natives are always willing to keep a sense of humor, which is an endearing characteristic. They manage humor in life and have fun, even when they're feeling low.

Capricorn Ascendant

There is an unmistakable seriousness to Capricorn rising natives. Even when they're kidding around, they do so in a deadpan way. Actually, there are quite a few humorous people who have Capricorn Ascendants. In fact, they have great timing, and they don't giggle before the joke is over.

Competence is the word that comes to mind when you think of Capricorn Ascendant people. They exude it. They are image-conscious and are very particular about the clothes they wear, and their way of presenting themselves to the world is a big deal to them. They want to present that they are successful.

In childhood, Capricorn Ascendants were the children who were considered the conscientious and responsible ones. Sometimes, they look around themselves and feel there is a need to be the dependable, capable, and structured members of their family. Capricorn rising natives take on the responsibility of their family at a young age.

Capricorn rising people are forever concerned about being secure for their dependents and themselves. Underneath the hard-working, dependable character with a cool exterior that they convey to the world is someone who is enmeshed in an inner struggle. They continually ask themselves if they're doing enough or if they deserve all that they have worked for, and they worry about the future.

If you look at Capricorn Ascendants and think their success has come easy, believe that it has not. They make it look easy, but they are hard-working, driven, and patient to get where they're going. Some Capricorn rising people do away with frivolous spending. However, they'll spend money on clothing that bears the right labels and those they really want and other status-symbol items. Showiness for them is rare, and their success is a result of conscious effort.

Capricorn rising people are, more often than not, people who become successful. They may have had difficult childhoods, but they have the ability to turn their lives around to achieve the success they want it to be.

Aquarius Ascendant

Aquarius rising natives can be described as original, unique, and just plain different, and they won't let you forget it. Aquarius rising people have savvy and intellectual aplomb and are often sought out for their advice. For these natives, there is an appeal for both metaphysics and science and an interest in the advancement of the human race.

The people with this sign are not easily shocked—they have seen or done it all or may want you to think that they have. They sometimes get a kick in shocking others. They're not flashy or gaudy by nature, but getting a rise out of others gives them a special glee. Some Aquarius on their Ascendant can be irreverent and provocative, albeit quietly.

Aquarian rising people are likable and friendly, and the quirks in their personalities are relatively accepted by others. They themselves give others freedom, and they view equality in people from all backgrounds. Their somewhat detached and cool curiosity about everything around them, whether it's the environment or the people, is appealing to others.

They are humanitarians and kind, but they can come across as somewhat standoffish. Some devote their humanitarianism to animals and children, and it isn't a surprise to find they contribute money and time to those causes.

Aquarius Ascendants feel special or different throughout their lives and have been labeled as original and independent as children. Some feel they exist on the "outside looking in" and their ability to surmise by observing is frequently uncanny.

They have the ability to get things to work, piecing together different things that didn't seem to work together, but do in the end. This works for them, particularly when it comes to groups of people, and it makes them good team leaders and managers.

Aquarius rising natives sometimes have an eccentricity to their manner, and some have an offbeat way of dressing. It may not be dressing to look or stand out like a sore thumb but enough to let them express their originality. Their choice of clothes shows how they present themselves to the world.

There is definitely a stubborn streak in these Aquarius rising people, which may surprise some who see this sign as open to new ideas. Aquarius is a fixed sign, and with Aquarius, there are those who will be resistant to change. This characteristic seems to contradict their generally forward-looking nature. There's a tendency to try and force their own opinions on others, and there's inflexibility with Aquarius rising natives.

Some Aquarius Ascendants, at times, ignore the needs of the people closest to them and are frequently attracted to those who possess passion and self-confidence.

Pisces Ascendant

Pisces rising has a motto that almost everyone, at one time or the other, has thought or said—go with the flow. They have a gentle, yet directionless manner. They move like this throughout the world. This description somewhat describes how a fish move through the water, gentle and directionless.

Pisces rising people have open hearts and minds and appear to others as artists and peace lovers. Yet they seem to have a chameleon-like persona. One is not quite sure which persona you'll have to interact with each time. One day, they may be passionate and talkative with everyone, and the next day, they will be shy and quiet.

Pisces Ascendants are impressionable, are soft-hearted, and can come across as dreamy. They're not objective and see the world in the way that they want to view it. They're not very objective when making decisions as well.

Pisces rising natives don't like to be labeled as any one thing. They don't want to be pinned or pegged in any way, as there is changeability in their characters. They are not happy living in any one way due to their restless nature that is constantly searching and changing. They don't have a plan that's solid or decisive for tomorrow or, for that matter, even today. They prefer to keep all options open. Structure and organization for them are rather limiting because, in their changing of their minds or what they want to do at any given time, they like to feel their way through life.

If you don't own a fish tank, go to an aquarium and watch how the fish glide in and out of all the caves and sea plants, heading one way one minute and then another way. This will give you an idea as to what goes on in a Pisces rising native's mind and way of being.

These people look for partnerships that are reliable and stable. Pisces rising natives are inclined to seek partners who are challenging. There seems to be a need for a realistic, practical partner.

Pisces Ascendants are sometimes prone to allergies and frequently have a drug sensitivity. Their physical constitution and the immune system seem to be less resistant than most.

Pisces rising natives, quite often, are blessed with a charm that's irresistible and a soft aura that surrounds them. This charm isn't loud, center-of-attention charm but one that is quiet in its own way. They intrigue others with their mannerisms and appearance.

Cusp Signs

Chapter 7: Are You Born on a Cusp?

When someone asks the question, "what's your sign?" they'll probably give you the one-word answer of Aquarius or Scorpio (although this Sun sign likes to be mysterious about it, so you may not get an answer), or Leo because we all know they are ruled by the Sun, the center of everything, pretty much Leo's personality.

But what about those individuals who were born on a cusp, i.e., being born under two signs? What about the duality of it all—that gray area when the Sun transitions out of one sign into the next one? Those born on the cusp may feel they have an identity dilemma and are affected by two different signs, which can sometimes be quite the opposite of one another.

Is it possible that a person born on the cusp is likely to retain the traits of both signs, even though they can only identify with one Sun sign?

The zone that identifies the cusp of each astrological sign is determined by the five days that surround the date that the sun officially transitions into the next sign.

For example, if you were born between April 19 and April 23, you are born on the cusp of Aries the Ram and Taurus the Bull. This can bring a fiery go-getter, quick quality of Aries to the otherwise slow, plodding of Taurus.

Even if you were born on the transitional day of two signs, such as October 24 when Libra moves into Scorpio, the person born on this day is either a Libra or, without a doubt, a Scorpio, so there's no reason to have to read two horoscopes like you do if you're reading not only your Sun sign but your Ascendant sign as well. It is helpful to check out both signs because it can be helpful if you're confused about the birth sign you identify with.

The birth on a cusp is complex, and each cusp is like a sign on its own, with the original 12 astrological signs becoming 24 in all. (Cafe Astrology staff, 2019)

Each of the following cusps is a guide of how a sign's planet and element affects the other.

Aries-Taurus Cusp (April 17–23) — The Cusp of Power

This cusp characterizes the natural leadership of Aries and the details from the disciplinarian Taurus, and don't forget how much quicker Taurus will move with the quickness of the Aries sign's influence.

Both the active Mars and the sensual lover of beauty, Venus, the planets that rule Aries and Taurus, influence those born on this cusp.

Mars is the planet of drive and motivation, while Venus epitomizes beauty and persuasion. This energy combination is a blend that is unstoppable on the way up to the goal of success.

Aries' element of Fire and the Taurean element of Earth mix together on this cusp to give you a personality that is brave yet grounded. There is the energy to advance in situations or projects and steadiness to see things through to completion. Remember to consider the project before you act so you don't get stuck in something, and you won't quit because of your stubbornness.

You know how to have fun and a good time while you make your way to the top if you're born on the Cusp of Power. You have outgoing social skills that can get you anywhere you wish. You can handle quite a bit; your thick skin helps with that. Your independence can sometimes detach you from those who love you. Don't let that happen because you do need them. Have patience. Realize that leaders who are kind can accomplish great things.

Strengths – Fun, smart, energetic, humorous, brave

Weaknesses – Self-centered, controlling, pushy, stubborn, insensitive

Taurus-Gemini Cusp (May 17–23) — The Cusp of Energy

Those born on the Taurus-Gemini cusp give you the dual bonus of having the physical strength and mental agility. This cusp is a social, youthful spirit.

The impact of the sensual, friendly Venus, ruler of Taurus, and the sociable and quick Mercury, ruler of Gemini, makes you rather the socialite. This mix of energy gives you the ability to easily make friends, as well as sustain great relationships. You love to talk; you are very clever, witty, and loving, which are qualities that make you very popular with all sorts of people.

The Taurean Earth sign, meeting the Gemini Air sign on the Cusp of Energy, creates quite a storm of activity. You have the ability to be both flexible and stable, depending on the situation. You are able to be adaptable and enjoy wherever you are. You have the endurance to accomplish all you want to and then do more if you want.

You are able to converse easily, and social settings are just the thing you like after a day of accomplishing your goals. It doesn't matter whether you're meeting someone new or catching up with a long-time friend; you are always fun and have something interesting to say. You love to have a fun night out, meeting friends at the newest restaurant in town. Something, like enjoying a concert or having a hot date with your partner, is what you feel life is all about. You burn the candle at both ends at times, and sometimes, it could get the better of you.

You're not unbeatable, and while it's true you're a fireball of energy, you tend to overdo it in drink and food, spending, physical activity, and not making time to get enough rest. Beware of the toll that the never-ending party can take on you, your health, and your finances. Enjoy yourself, but be smart and careful in what you do.

Your energy and exciting nature inspire others, and your smooth-talking is persuasive.

Give others an opportunity to have the spotlight every now and then. You're sometimes so busy socializing and chatting that you forget to share the limelight. You are charismatic, so much so that there are those who would love to have that ability. Make sure that you use your charisma with poise and dignity. You'll build fulfilling friendships for a lifetime.

Strengths – Fun, adaptable, amusing, charming, energetic, sociable

Weaknesses – Reckless, impatient, self-absorbed, wild, lenient, brash

Gemini-Cancer Cusp (June 18–24) — The Cusp of Magic

A kind, fanciful, and fun person with a gigantic heart is a person born on the Gemini-Cancer cusp, the Cusp of Magic. Your childlike and loving manner will afford you a continuously happy life.

Quick and curious Mercury, the planet ruling of Gemini and emotional Moon, the planet ruling Cancer are a combination of energies that make you sociable and enable you to have durable relationships. Your interest in others is sincere, and you really want to know how someone feels when you ask them how they are.

The Air sign, Gemini's element, fills you with curiosity, and the Water sign, Cancer's element, gives you a sense of sentimentality. Air and Water can combine and be fun, but they can also overwhelm you. You have sensitivity and empathy, but they can overflow if you aren't logical and you don't keep things in perspective. Balancing these energies will help you to be a perceptive and emotionally intelligent friend for your partner, family, and friends.

Communication is a gift that comes from being born on the Cusp of Magic because you are a good listener and communicator. Sharing witty and interesting stories, or being a sounding board for a loved one who needs some advice, you handle yourself elegantly with any group. People confide in you, and, although you are a dedicated conversationalist, you have difficulty sharing your feelings with others. It doesn't come as easily as others who share their feelings with you.

You appear to be easy and carefree on the exterior, but your inner self may be a wound-up ball of tension. You're very sensitive, and you soak up the emotions and feelings of others. You lack trust in people and urge people to talk about themselves or interact with others in relaxed conversation to evade talking about yourself and your own issues. Having a partner will help you handle your problems rather than attempt to handle them alone.

You are cared for, and the people around you are extremely supportive. Don't fear to talk about your own issues. It's the emotional balance you need to live a contented and happy life.

Strengths – Flirty, fun, affectionate, intellectual, curious, dedicated, sensitive, inspiring

Weaknesses – Emotional, moody, depressive, flighty, self-absorbed, self-destructive

Cancer-Leo Cusp (July 19–25) — The Cusp of Oscillation

Let's begin with the word oscillation. According to Merriam-Webster, the meaning is a fluctuation between beliefs, opinions, and conditions. Now that there's clarity about the definition, it somewhat explains the Cancer-Leo cusp.

Those born on the Cancer-Leo cusp have a vast range of personality characteristics that will make or break these individuals. Born on the Cusp of Oscillations, this makes for a very influential and powerful person.

These two very different zodiac signs—Cancer ruled by the emotional, sensitive Moon, and Leo, the brave and proud sign ruled by the impassioned Sun—can be affected by both the Moon and the Sun, which can be advantageous but challenging as well. Learning to fluctuate between these two energies, you'll be able to feel and understand your emotions, as well as the emotions of others. You'll learn how to articulate and act on them applicably.

People born on this cusp have two very different elements of Cancer's Water and Leo's Fire. This combination can create scorching steam! Your mood may switch from a melodramatic queen to a sensitive and shy individual. The element of

Water underlines your emotions, yet Fire can bring on these unpredictable moments. Taking action with your feelings is fine, as long as they're channeled into love and not hostility or self-protectiveness.

You're a leader and a lover when born on the Cusp of Oscillation, helping you to be both persuasive and powerful. You have an honest interest and empathy for others, which gives you the ability to bond with people easily. You can be ready to lead once you've won their trust.

You are a wonderful combination of being passionate and caring, and you can use the energy to assist others in need or bring awareness to good causes. Your emotional perception and charisma give you the capability of motivating people and having them do as you ask. Be careful to use this for good and not your personal gain.

You'll find that people are easily influenced by you. When the Sun and Moon planets are balanced and in sync, you'll do incredible things that help others and for the greater good. But, if the energies are out of sync, and the Moon sensitivity or the dramatic Sun are overpowering you, you may be motivated to manipulate the situation or others.

Those born on the Cancer-Leo cusp have the ability to be a versatile, effective individual. Two vastly different signs are your influence, and it will take a bit of work on your part to keep these two energies balanced and in sync, instead of against one another.

When you merge your confidence in yourself with your empathy and care for others, you can become a deeply respected, successful leader. It is fulfilling to devote your time to assisting others and creating a positive difference. Balance these two signs and their elements, and you will accomplish incredible things.

Strengths – Dedicated, creative, loving, passionate, sensitive

Weaknesses – Overly sensitive, melodramatic, volatile, self-absorbed, dependent

Leo-Virgo Cusp (August 19–25) — The Cusp of Exposure

You have a vision for the world, you are a natural leader, and you have the capability to command a room if you are born on the Leo-Virgo Cusp. Born on the Cusp of Exposure, with your balance in sync, your destiny is to be a success.

Born on this Cusp, the Sun, Leo's ruling planet, and Mercury, Virgo's ruling planet, influence your characteristics of being big and bright. You are able to think, process, and speak about all the tiny details. Both these elements are strong forces that have you both thinking intensely and acting in a big way. Balancing these two elements is important to find harmony.

These two elements, the passion, and intensity of the Fire sign of Leo, and the durability of the Earth sign of Virgo can be extremely complex to blend. The good news is that you can charm anyone. You have a charisma that is childlike in nature, and you are loyal to those whom you trust.

You have lofty standards, and it's a wonder that anyone meets or exceeds your expectations. However, those who do are compensated by your appreciation and praise, making you a great leader, as long as you stay modest and gracious in the success you achieve.

Although your impressive energy may be inspiring to some, being born on the Cusp of Exposure has you running the risk of becoming bossy and domineering. There is a delicate balance that needs to be maintained between these two elements. You're very smart, yet it's up to you to remain humble and diplomatic about it. Don't show off your braininess and go around making corrections of others' work. You may lose the respect you've worked hard to achieve.

You see the goals and the big picture and have the ability to reduce them down to the smallest of details, delineating which steps need to be taken to reach those goals. You can be smart and charming or rude, loud, and bossy. The balance of this cusp needs to happen, not to lean too far on one side or the other.

Maintain a healthy balance, and be the humble, gentle, and motivated person that you can be to achieve your goals.

Strengths – Passionate, loyal, honest, hardworking, responsible, successful

Weaknesses – Stubborn, argumentative, critical, controlling, manipulative, brusque

Virgo-Libra Cusp (September 19–25) — The Cusp of Beauty

Beautiful inside and out is the person born on the Virgo-Libra Cusp. Born on the Cusp of Beauty, you are balanced, graceful, and a vision of perfection.

People born on the Virgo-Libra Cusp are influenced by Virgo's ruling planet, Mercury, and Libra's ruling planet of Venus. They have charm and wit. This combination can make you incredibly persuasive if you use it correctly.

The Earth sign of Virgo gives you grounded determination, and the social charisma and ease of the Air sign Libra make this mix of elements a blissful, happy one. Your understanding of the world is realistic, and you share your thoughts articulately and fairly. You are extremely well-liked.

You are generous and elegant, and, no matter how you look, you're an air of loveliness. You're beloved by family and friends, as well as all those who have the chance to be enchanted by your gentle heart and kind words. You abhor cruelty and admire all those who fight for equality.

Although you usually are calm and cool, you do easily get upset when your standards are not met by others, and the bar is set pretty high. If someone tells a joke that is crass or vulgar, they will hear your disdain rather quickly. You cringe at that type of behavior. However, be careful not to stick your nose up too high. People are prone to mistakes and need to have the opportunity to be human. No one is perfect. Loosening your perfectionist attitudes and learning to breathe will make others inspired by your example.

Strengths – Intelligent, attractive, communicative, artistic, sensuous, social

Weaknesses – Materialistic, detached, perfectionist, superficial, jaded

Libra-Scorpio Cusp (October 19–25) — The Cusp of Drama

People born under this cusp draw people in and spew them out just as fast. This is the persona of those born on the Cusp of Drama and Criticism, and you excel at both.

You're influenced by two appealing and commanding planets—ruling planet of Venus, the planet of beauty and love, and Scorpio's ruling planet of Pluto, the dark and mysterious planet renowned for its passion and depth. Individuals born on this cusp are magnetic and, whether you know it or not, has the ability of seduction.

Libra's Air element and Scorpio's Water element meet on the Cusp of Drama and Criticism, and they can be cool and calm or a dangerous storm. Regardless of whether you are an extrovert or an introvert, you have a storm rumbling internally in your heart and your head. Total honesty and truth are the only things that give you a feeling of being settled.

People appreciate your frankness even if they seem daunted by you. There is rarely a gray area with you—right and wrong are black and white, and you don't hesitate to voice your opinion when something is unjust. You're intelligent and watchful, so you see things rather quickly while it may take others a while to catch on. Have some patience when articulating your judgment; you may drive everyone away otherwise.

You abhor liars and dishonesty, and it's hard to allow others in because of your mistrust of people. You still desire relationships because of your emotional makeup. Don't be afraid to let people in. You just need to trust your intuition about others.

People born on this cusp have magnetism and charm that essentially give you control over any situation. You will go deep to learn the truth and get reasonable results. You are judgmental due to your ability to see right from wrong. Learn to be more open-minded to have true relationships and lead a satisfying life.

Strengths – Competent, powerful, charming, intelligent, honest, provocative

Weaknesses – Sarcastic, harsh, pessimistic, critical, isolated

Scorpio-Sagittarius Cusp (November 18–24) — The Cusp of Revolution

Those born on the Scorpio-Sagittarius cusp have a source of incredible power and strength, born on the Cusp of the Revolution. This makes you capable and passionate, and you will stand up for your beliefs and fight for them.

Born on this cusp, Scorpio's planet of Pluto is the planet of death and Sagittarius' ruling planet of Jupiter, the planet of rebirth, are your influences. They inspire you to accept your personal power and right any wrongs. This is a combination of transformation and motivation that makes you so revolutionary.

You are fortunate with a Water sign, Scorpio, and the exhilaration of a Fire sign, Sagittarius, which gives you a vast array of abilities. This mix of friendliness and empathy is what makes you extremely generous. Be aware of those who look to take advantage of your charitable nature.

Those born on the Cusp of Revolution are strong and ready for action to motivate and lead. You stand by your convictions, and your sociable, magnetic attitude will have you accomplishing significant things in life.

However, a lack of freedom is something that will frustrate you and will hold you back. It would be wise to look for opportunities that will give you the independence you need.

Those born on the Scorpio-Sagittarius cusp are practical and can be somewhat rebellious. Although you like to stir the pot, others may not appreciate this, and the energy you exude can be a bit too much for some. Your energy can also make you seem standoffish or overbearing, frequently misunderstood by others. They aren't sure which person will emerge when they see you—fun and flexible or complex and fierce.

You aren't afraid to express yourself and speak your mind. You have solid standards and beliefs. You flourish with those around you who share your vivacity and strength and who can withstand you rubbing them the wrong way. You've had experience in ruffling some feathers.

You can accomplish great things with your strength and independence. These attributes can also lead to conflicts in relationships and authority figures. Direct your fierceness into determination rather than aggression, and you will go far.

Strengths – Adventurous, accomplished, energetic, passionate, benevolent

Weaknesses – Secretive, rebellious, aggressive, selfish, brusque, misunderstood

Sagittarius-Capricorn Cusp (December 28–24) — The Cusp of Prophecy

Those born on the Sagittarius-Capricorn cusp are visionaries who will achieve certain success. Born on the Cusp of Prophecy, your resilient will, and forceful determination will get you where you want to go.

Your passion is fueled by Sagittarius' element of Fire, and Capricorn's element of Earth pushes you forward with intense stubbornness. The element of Fire assists your positive thinking and excitement about life, but when the fire dies out, your Earth element gives you the endurance you need to get things done and completed.

Those born on Sagittarius-Capricorn cusp are caring, loyal, and social. There will always be people surrounding you who care and admire you and want to know what you have to say and what you think. You have a strong suit to teach others, as long as you don't become impatient or belligerent with people who learn at a slower pace.

You are a hardworking person who wants to prosper and succeed. You are motivated and want to climb to the top. However, take care because your concentrated focus can develop a division between you and those you love. You may end up lonely because your uncompromising and independent attitude is too busy changing the world.

You have all the possibilities you can imagine at your fingertips if you're born on the Cusp of Prophecy. Be appreciative of the determination and natural energy that is your gift, but use it for good.

An honest difference can be made by you as long as there's a plan to get where you're going. You'll be the leader and teacher you were meant to be if you remember to show concern for others and enjoy yourself on the way to the top.

Strengths – Responsible, friendly, loyal, successful, humorous

Weaknesses – Impatient, uncooperative, selfish, moody, closed, intense

Capricorn-Aquarius Cusp (January 17–23) — The Cusp of Mystery and Imagination

Those born on the cusp of Capricorn possess contrasting energies that make you distinctive and unique. Born on the Cusp of Mystery and Imagination, you are a hardworking optimist.

These signs of Capricorn and Aquarius are very different. However, the combination provides the ability to see the world in an unequaled way. The planet of lessons and limits, Capricorn's ruling planet Saturn, urges you to have a practical look at life and take care of your real-world obligations. Adversely, Aquarius' ruling planet of Uranus leads you to have an open mind of others around you. Blended together, these two abilities can make for a creative, striving, and potently brilliant person.

The two elements, Capricorn's Earth, determined and stable, and Aquarius' Air, desire spontaneity and variety. The challenge for you is to tend to both sides of your personality. If your energies can be channeled properly, you'll be able to succeed in any situation.

There is quite a bit of excitement internally for those born on the Cusp of Mystery and Imagination. Your mind is always racing and rolling out ideas and thoughts that are interesting. Be aware, however, that you may seem to be uninterested or detached by situations and people around you because of the continual dreams and fantasies streaming through your mind.

You love to have stimulating conversations, and people enjoy talking with you. You love to talk about problems and how there are ways to fix them. This may make you a fascinating communicator and conversationalist, but when it comes to catching up with those who care about you, it can be isolating and intimidating.

Don't forget to check in with those family and friends to see how they're doing while you share your opinions about issues regarding the world with others.

When you aren't working hard with your social networks and creative ideas that bring purpose and exhilaration to your life, remember that even the best of ideas need support from those around you who are supportive. Put extra time and effort into bonding and appreciating the people in your life.

Strengths – Creative, determined, idealistic, compassionate, entertaining

Weaknesses – Detached, selfish, standoffish, chaotic, disapproving

Aquarius-Pisces Cusp (February 15–21) — The Cusp of Sensitivity

Those born on the Aquarius-Pisces cusp are full of creativity and compassion and are blessed and cursed by feeling the weight of the world.

The Aquarius-Pisces cusp feels Aquarius' ruling planet of Uranus that brings out the progressive energy and your eccentricity, as well as Pisces' ruling planet of Neptune that advocates the acceptance of your imagination and dreams.

The Aquarius-Pisces cusp individual is friendly, peace-loving, spiritual, artistic, and extremely original. This cusp is usually labeled as eccentric or unconventional. You have a high intellect, but you can be a bit scattered and not good with follow-through and details. You are intensely intuitive and probing into philosophical ideals and matters of the spiritual nature are more significant than taking care of the details of daily life.

You are very sensitive, especially to the world around you, yet you're very strong emotionally. You're in tune with others around you, and you are in tune with their needs, hopes, fears, and feelings. The Aquarius humanitarianism, blended with the empathetic Pisces, takes understanding and compassion to a higher level.

You soak up the feelings of the people around you and have a real need to help others. Just remember to take care of your own needs and feelings as well.

Sometimes the feelings and emotions of the world can be harmful and can make you feel overwhelmed or depressed. Give yourself the same love you give to others.

Strengths – Empathetic, generous, intuitive, creative, understanding

Weaknesses – Isolated, depressed, detached, insecure

Pisces-Aries Cusp (March 17–23) — The Cusp of Rebirth

Those born on the Pisces-Aries cusp are dreamers and go-getters all rolled into one! The last sign of the Zodiac is Pisces, and the first sign of the Zodiac is Aries, thus making this the Cusp of Rebirth. You are impulsive and imaginative, and you know what you want and want it immediately, if not sooner!

The Cusp of Rebirth is influenced by Pisces' ruling planet, the fantastical Neptune, and Aries' ruling planet, Mars. Neptune heightens your imagination, and you'll get motivated with an initiative with active Mars. You are an individual who is creative and takes the dreams you have and put them into action. Your wishes become your realities because you know how to make them come true.

The empathy and intuition of Pisces' element of Water and Aries' element of Fire are a steamy mix. Your emotions are deep, as are your beliefs, and you want to share them with the world. Not everyone thinks the way you do, so if others don't agree with you, don't take it personally.

Born on the Pisces-Aries cusp, you're strong and instinctive. This combination of energy gives you the opportunity to combine your compassion for others. You can become a successful leader because of this blend of energies. Your friends and associates will know your loyalty, and there can be some who will climb to the top with you.

You can be impatient, and your impulsiveness is joined with your intuitive knowledge. Your impulsiveness, sometimes, does not allow you to think things out, and you get into action as soon as your ideas come to you.

Your birth on the Cusp of Rebirth provides you with an ardent imagination that lets you create different and new stories, theories, and opinions. You are an ingenious pioneer who takes the best arrangement and understands the needs of others. Concentrate your energy and use the abilities you have wisely. You will be an impressive force of nature to reckon with.

Strengths – Driven, intuitive, smart, creative, quirky, fun

Weaknesses - Impulsive, selfish, uncompromising, stubborn

Love in the Stars

Chapter 8: Are You Compatible?

Love is a powerful emotion and one of the reasons that make astrology popular with people who want to better understand their love compatibility. We, as human beings, have sought love in one another for many reasons.

Many of us look for true love that will complete us and be our one and only match, while others approach love and its power differently and believe in many loves; that it is not the love of another that completes us but the love for ourselves.

These different approaches can be explained by understanding the astrological love sign and investigate what answers the stars give us at the time of our birth.

Astrology can reveal quite a bit about who we are and how we relate to others. This is significant to know when delving a horoscope compatibility love match.

A great tool for helping you find the right love for you is the Zodiac love compatibility tool. It can help you learn why you are attracted to one person and not another, even though they may both have all the things you look for in a romantic partner. Your love horoscope compatibility may be the answer as to why that intense desire or special spark is missing.

Astrology and its complexities help make love compatibility a science. The answer lies in the astrologers and those of us who look to the stars.

Love Secrets of Venus

The sign position of Venus discloses the "role" we take on when we want to entice love. However, it goes beyond just flirtation, and we do not "act" or facilitate a show. The traits of our Venus sign are honest traits that come from within. They are highlighted and strongly activated when we are in love.

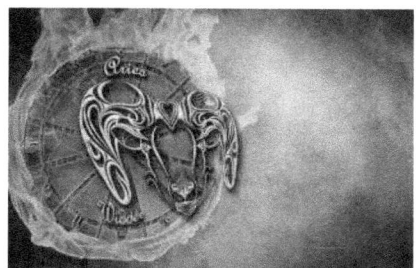

Venus in Aries

Venus in Aries people do their flirting by being direct, daring, and up-front. They express how independent and resourceful they are and try to win you over with this information. Their style of expressing love can be "me-centered," which can be maddening. However, the right person will find this charming. Aries' aura of childishness and impatience and the aura of innocent charm are things that turn some people on.

Women and men with Venus in Aries have a fun-loving, childlike manner in love. They love activity and energy and are turned on by both. The turn-offs are relationships that they consider too "mature" or stuffy, ducking the issues and being too vague. Venus in Aries people are utterly addicted to the conquest when they're in love. They need a lot of stimulation for a relationship to retain its freshness.

In order to please Venus in Aries, their need for action has to be fueled. Be open, honest and direct with them. Unless it's for fun, they're not going to play games or evasiveness. Their need for spontaneity and playfulness needs to be appreciated. Acknowledge their wish for wanting the relationship to remain fresh and young.

Pander to their many whims, and understand that they flourish on competition, even if they're competing with you.

Venus in Taurus

Love for Venus in Taurus encompasses creature comforts and the physical world. They adore their surroundings to be sensual. They express themselves as comfortable and solid. There is something about their way that promises they will be pleasing partners and lovers. In their relationships, they need a particular measure of dependability and predictability.

Women and men with Venus in Taurus have a tendency to be possessive in love and are threatened by high-energy situations in the framework of love and relationships. There are lots of expressions of love for this sensual Venus in Taurus. Their lovers may grumble about becoming a little too settled and comfortable. They do struggle with change in their relationships, but even when they seem wedged in a groove, there is always the reassurance that Venus in Taurus partners are constant.

In order to please Venus in Taurus, you need to emphasize their worth to you and your loyalty to them. They won't readily give in to you in the matters of love, so just give up and give in to them. Do comfortable things and get physical with them. Give them time to fall in love; there's no need to push them. Learn to develop patience if you're in a relationship with Venus in Taurus. Be natural and simple; promise them a cozy, comfortable time. They'll appreciate it.

Venus in Gemini

Venus in Gemini people will display how much they know to exhibit their varied interests and will try to win over the love interest with witty conversation. They are playful lovers, and some might say they like to tease. They're not easy to pin down and have a resistance to relationships that become too comfortable.

Women and men with Venus in Gemini are not in the market to become bogged or tied down in their relationships. The type of love they appreciate is lighthearted. You may get the feeling that although they will talk about the relationship, they'll avoid the deeper issues.

Their tastes change from one day to the next or, in some cases, from one hour to the next! It can be hard to know what to expect. Remember, Gemini is the Twin Sign of the Zodiac, and it doesn't necessarily mean that the twins are identical. And be aware that each "twin" may have another twin. You are forewarned!

In order to please Venus in Gemini, show interest in their knowledge and braininess, giving them their space for activities and friends outside the relationship and their need for variety and fun. Tell them how much fun they are and that you have fun with them. Don't get overly annoyed by Venus in Gemini's fickle, changeable ways. Time spent with your lover will be stimulating and exciting.

Venus in Cancer

Love for Venus in Cancer is predictable and best when it is committed. They are sensitive in love. Their egos are a bit underdeveloped when it comes to love, but they have care, comfort, and security to give.

Women and men with Venus in Cancer exhibit their love by caring for you. Their attention is more on your feelings than your words, and they watch you pretty carefully. They want a solid, safe relationship. There are times they can give you the silent treatment and be moody, using pouting routines for attention. Anything impersonal turns them off, and you leave them cold with too much explaining and rationalizing. Confrontation doesn't frighten them. Yet, they get worried about being left alone. There are times when they'll withdraw, and it can take a while and some work to pull them out.

To please Venus in Cancer, it takes a lot of sentimentality and cuddling. Acknowledge their attachments to home and family. Always make them feel cared for and secure, and they will reward you with a dependable, patient, and loving partner.

Venus in Leo

Venus in Leo people are boastful and proud to be in love. Venus in Leo loves to be courted and needs to feel exclusive. They are impressive, generous, and warm. Love is the most important in Leo's life, and they are very loyal to their partners. They blossom on romantic attention. They will tell you about anyone who makes advances on them, but you do not need to worry; they're just showing off their allure, and it's most likely harmless. However, don't do the same thing. That's when Leo the Lion will roar.

Women and men with Venus in Leo are quite big-hearted about almost everything. They do have high expectations. If the relationship has settled too much or lost the spark, they'll feel threatened. If you are indifferent or impersonal in your attitude toward them, they will feel threatened as well.

Pleasing Venus in Leo has you paying quite a bit of attention toward them. Remind yourself to let Leo know how wonderful they are. Do this daily. Appreciate and respect them. They tend to lose interest when they sense a loss of interest from their partner. Remind them that you have feelings, and your emotions count as well. When Venus in Leo feels appreciated and loved, you will be rewarded with their loyalty, plenty of physical expressions of their love, and a great sense of fun.

Venus in Virgo

Venus in Virgo people have an appeal that lies in their inclination to work on a relationship and make it work in real terms. They won't try to impress you with impressive promises or gifts. Their gifts are those of commitment and attention to you.

Women and men with Venus in Virgo slowly and quietly make their way into your heart. They are somewhat insecure and very sensitive, and this loner-like quality is part of their appeal. They need to feel confident that you like them before they make any moves, and they would prefer to play it safe in their relationships. They learn all your idiosyncrasies and are great listeners. They sometimes display their love by criticizing and nagging. Although they're calling out the flaws in your thinking, plans, or character, they're not trying to hurt you. They are actually trying to help.

To please Venus in Virgo, you need to show appreciation for all the things they do, and they do quite a bit. They do things quietly, and you may not really notice and give them credit. They appreciate being given some space, so give it to them; they'll thank you for it. Be real, not affected or showy. Take care of their basic needs, and you'll find they're pretty easy to please. They're shy, so take it a step at a time in introducing them to your family or friends. They like to please and can be easily intimidated by the experiences you've had. Express how much you value and appreciate them, and you'll be rewarded with devotion.

Venus in Libra

Venus in Libra people will try to make an impression by being willing to make your relationship work, their impartiality, and their kindness. Theirs is a manner of love that is polished, which can appear to be superficial or disingenuous. They treat love gently and don't like being offended. They are intimidated by a direct or abrasive exhibition of feelings and by bad manners. They look for the middle ground in their relationships. Venus in Libra's way to accommodate you by adjusting their lives may turn you on, and you can always expect to be treated fairly.

Women and men with Venus in Libra have views of their relationships that are idealized. If they feel they are being taken advantage of, they can become resentful. They make it easy for someone who is more aggressive to bully them around.

In order to please Venus in Libra, you need to treat them fairly and with kindness. Let them share everything with you. They love to converse with you about the relationship, so foreplay may be mental. They get turned on by sharing and turned off by uncouth or insensitive behavior. An imbalance in the relationship will make them unhappy, and they may have a subtle way of getting even. Don't let your relationship become imbalanced, and you will gain a reward with a lover who treats you exactly how they would like to be treated.

Venus in Scorpio

Venus in Scorpio people have been willing to commit; they are very intense, which draws others to them. Their feeling runs deep. Their promise of sexual pleasure and deep commitment will be revealed to you in their actions rather than their words. Their appeal is in their dedication and focus on you. They are fearless in being intimate, and a potential lover will feel as if they will never look elsewhere. They are extremely loyal to the person they love. They make it extremely attractive to be possessed.

Women and men with Venus in Scorpio give you their undivided and complete attention. They are focused on their partners. You may find this trait either entirely flattering or unsettling. Their need to control their partner is strong, but it won't be immediately obvious, and they may not confess to this. This may make loving them a burdensome experience because of the intensity of commitment and love. If you're looking for a lighthearted relationship, this isn't the one for you. They can be provocative and take things to extremes. They like exploring and knowing all about you but aren't as forthcoming about themselves. If they become upset with you, you won't have to guess—they'll be happy to let you know. Be aware that they're not fearful of being devious when it comes to matters of the heart and are specialists in cutting through the nonsense and see you for who and what you are. You may find their assumptions a bit mistrustful.

In order to please Venus in Scorpio, you need to exhibit your loyalty and entire commitment to them. If it's possible and you feel they are deserving, let go of some of the control in the relationship. Give them the feeling they own you; just don't allow it to go to extremes. However, Venus in Scorpio lovers will be understated in the ways they take advantage of you to keep you all to themselves. Allow them their quietness and mystery.

Venus in Sagittarius

Venus in Sagittarius people need to feel they can increase their horizons and grow through their relationship when they are in love. They want new experiences and learn new things together with you. They want you to realize their ideals, beliefs, and visions. They don't commit as easily as others in their relationships.

Women and men with Venus in Sagittarius draw others to them with their laughs and smiles, jokes, their dreams, and their friendly, playful manner. They have open minds and are proud of that fact, but they can be judgmental as well.

If their lover is dull, has inhibitions, and is over-emotional, they feel threatened. When the relationship hits rough spots, they have the urge to run the other way. They need to get out and do something that's new before they return, but sometimes, their exit can be for good. Their attraction to people is for those who are in love with life.

In order to please Venus in Sagittarius, give them plenty of room to grow in the relationship. Learn to laugh, but don't laugh at their rants and tirades. Evade criticizing their principles, philosophizing with them, and joining them in debates. Don't force them to commit or corner them.

Venus in Capricorn

Venus in Capricorn people will display their responsible manner, self-control, and presence of mind, which is how they'll try to win your heart. They are savvy, controlled, and goal-oriented, and they want you to know it. They're careful in love, and some degree of expectedness is what they like.

Women and men Venus in Capricorn project an air of being capable, and their reclusiveness can be appealing. Venus in Capricorn can be a bit too deliberate and practical, and their lovers may grumble about that. They can give the impression that they're not spontaneous and lack warmth. Actually, they can be a romantic who desires a mate to share their lives with. They are attracted to goal-oriented and serious lovers.

In order to please a Venus in Capricorn, you need to show them you're realistic and sensible. They want to make an impression on you with the things they do.

They'll like to show you off to their family and friends and let you know you're a keeper.

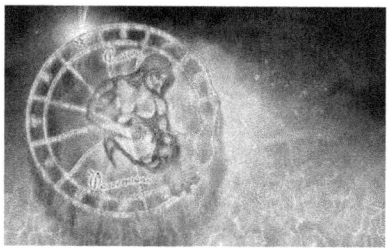

Venus in Aquarius

Venus in Aquarius people want to make an impression on you with their futuristic thinking and open-minded spirit. They want you to realize that they're a bit provocative, rebellious, and unique. When they're acting standoffish, they're attractive. In matters of love and the heart, they want you to know they follow the beat of a different drummer.

Women and men with Venus in Aquarius are enticed by eccentric or unusual relationships. They are not followers of the rule, yet they make a few of their own. They don't like restrictions of any kind and can appear to be aloof at times. Lovers who are the emotional type are not their cup of tea. They want to be loved for their intellect and to approve of their visions. They shun displays that are too emotional or confrontational. Venus in Aquarius will take pleasure in shocking you with their forward-looking thinking and curious ways.

When you want to please Venus in Aquarius, you need to tell them how intriguing they are. Accommodate their sporadic need to act lofty on an intellectual level. They take pride in their distinctive visions and ideas. Don't repress them or fence them in. Instead, dream along with them. They need breathing space, and they'll be very happy to give you lots of room to breathe, so you can be yourself.

Venus in Pisces

Venus in Pisces is a sensitive and dreamy partner. The way they flirt promises a delightful time. They can be playful, irregular, and a bit moody, and their charm is elusive. They value poetry and romance and like to explore both the relationship you share and you, so don't expect planning ahead. They are sensitive, and that sensitivity is directed toward all mankind, as well as themselves.

Women and men with Venus in Pisces give love unconditionally. They are not impressed by any status you may or may not have, and they accept and love you for who you are inside. They are attracted to rebellious souls and love the "runners up." With their romantic views, they can find states of martyrdom and suffering appealing. Pisces like inequality; it turns them on! They find it difficult to commit as much as they want to.

In order to please Venus in Pisces, enjoying romantic times and tender moments with them are things they like. They may stretch the truth occasionally and do so because they don't like to hurt you. Try to recognize that about them although it won't always be easy. They won't always be dependable. Some Venus in Pisces will have a love affair with the impression that they may be misunderstood. They are receptive and open to all options, and that makes it difficult for them to make a commitment to any idea, thing, or person. These partners are intriguing and will recompense you with a love that comes close to unconditional as anyone can get.

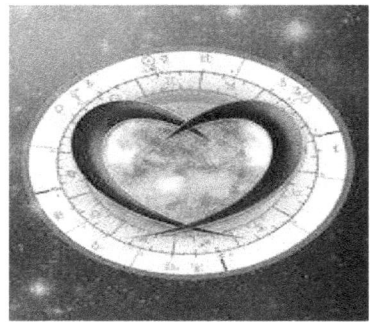

Chapter 9: How to Read Your Daily Horoscope

Are you one of those people who sit down with a cup of coffee, tea, orange juice, or a power drink, opens the newspaper or pops open the tablet or phone, and reads your horoscope to see what your future will be for the day?

Well, you're not alone because there are quite a few people who do the same thing. Approximately 70% of the population read their horoscope every day. Some may even read more than one horoscope. They may read it from more than one publication or website. (Schwimmer, Larry, 2015)

Why Do People Read Their Horoscope?

People read their horoscope for several reasons. Some people read it because they do believe that astrology is a predictor of their future. Some read it just for fun. Regardless of the reason that they read their horoscope, approximately 90% are not reading it correctly.

Most people reading their horoscope know what their Sun Sign is based on their birthdate. Every day, they go to their favorite horoscope website, newspaper, or magazine and read what's written for the Sun Sign.

If they're a Leo, they look up their Leo Sun Sign and read what the horoscope for that sign is for the day. That's it. They ponder on what they've read, and they move on to the next thing going on in their life.

This is not the way to read your horoscope. You have read only one aspect of your horoscope. You're not reading about your whole self. The Sun Sign applies to not only you but millions of other people. It's someone else's life you are reading about.

This may be a bit confusing, but the fact of the matter is, there are more signs that come into play in your astrological (natal) chart that is an integral part of who you are and lend themselves specifically to your horoscope.

Reading about your Sun Sign in the horoscope is reading the basics. You're reading about your identity but only a segment of it. The information you're receiving is valuable and covers the themes that are general and happening for all those who share your Sun Sign. Sun Sign astrology is used to develop a daily Horoscope for all the media outlets, websites, and periodicals to draw readers.

Let's face it; there are millions of people who share your Sun Sign. They can't all be having the same experience that you're having. They're reading the same horoscope that you are, but they are not the same as you and vice versa. Yes, you're all born under the same Sun Sign, but there are different aspects of your astrological makeup that precludes them from having the exact same experience that you have any day of the week, month, or year. It's not possible, and any astrologer who professionally draws astrological charts and has a full understanding of the art of astrology would never suggest otherwise. The horoscope that is available every day is limited in depth and range, making them far from accurate.

How Are Horoscopes Created?

Sun Sign horoscopes are made of four elements, as we have mentioned earlier. These are:
- The 12 Signs of the Zodiac
- The Planets
- The Houses
- The Planetary Aspects

There are 12 houses in a horoscope chart. Each House has a sign that rules that House. To determine which sign begins the First House of an astrological chart, the exact time of birth is necessary.

Sun Sin astrology analysis (these are the horoscope columns that everyone reads each morning) does not necessitate an exact time, and it's not used. The Sun Sign is put at the beginning of the chart, the First House, to be interpreted.

When reading a horoscope for your Sun Sign, (e.g., Taurus), you assume the sign ruling the First House is Taurus, and the Second House would be Gemini, and the Third House Cancer, etc.

However, if your Rising Sign is Leo, according to your exact birth time, your First House is in Leo, and reading a Taurus horoscope is not the horoscope that applies to you. The horoscope for Leo is the one that does. The events written for that day will probably fit you more rather than the general Sun Sign horoscope. (Schwimmer, Larry, 2015)

The Correct Way to Read Your Horoscope

The horoscope that you read each day is based on your Sun Sign, which is established solely on your birth date, which is pretty general. You can have a more well-rounded and accurate description of your horoscope if you know your Rising Sign.

If you don't know your Rising Sign, you can find it by using your birthday (month-day-year), your exact time of birth, and the city, state, and country of birth. The Rising Sign is established where the Ascendant (rising sign) is at the 9 o'clock position of your horoscope. It is the beginning of the entire chart.

The sign at this 9 o'clock position, which is your Rising Sign, is at the cusp of the First House. The degree and sign of your Rising Sign will determine the structure of the rest of your horoscope chart.

If you want to read your "complete" horoscope daily, you need to know your Rising Sign. For example, if you're a Taurus and your Rising Sun is in Leo, the more accurate reading and interpretation of your horoscope would be by reading the horoscope for Leo, not Taurus. You can read the Taurus Sun Sign, but remember that your Rising Sign makes the difference between you and the millions of others born under your Sun Sign.

What About Your Sun Sign?

So in reading the horoscope for your Rising Sign, does it negate your reading of your Sun Sign and its importance to your horoscope forecast? No, it doesn't! Actually, the best way to read any horoscope is to combine the two horoscope forecasts and blend them into your day-to-day reality.

Your Sun Sign will offer important information about general themes, an overview of what's happening for you. The Rising Sign horoscope is what will give you more for the timing of when things will occur with better accuracy. (Maria DeSiimone, 2019)

In order to totally understand yourself and events that may happen to you in your life, the accuracy of having a consultation and natal chart drawn by a professional astrologer is a good way to accomplish this.

Your chart can be interpreted and explained to you by a qualified astrologer. Major changes that will be happening in your life can be more accurately forecast by a natal chart reading. The astrological chart is like a map that is unique to you. Everyone should consider having their chart created at least once in their life.

Chapter 10: The Effect of Astrology on Different Religions and Cultures

Are there religions and cultures where astrology is based on? There are other cultures that do have their own zodiac that use the planets and signs to base their zodiac on.

The Chinese Zodiac

The Chinese zodiac is a significant element to the Chinese culture. For a very long time, the signs have been used as a way of dating years in a 12-YEAR cycle of the Chinese calendar. The significance of the zodiac to the Chinese culture is that folklore and stories have had animal signs used, which have created the different traits of their personality.

Today, millions of the people in China believe these "superstitions," these predictions that are defined within the Chinese zodiac.

Using this zodiac had led some to find their partners and friends with zodiac signs compatible with their own. It has also been used to see whom they get along with and work best with.

Generally, the Chinese zodiac provides direction on how people live and conduct their lives. In influencing the community and culture of China, the Chinese zodiac plays a significant and fascinating role.

Effects on Relationships

Relationships, from friends to mates and even business associates, are based on the Chinese zodiac. Some search for others whose zodiac sign are compatible with theirs—someone they would get along with, according to the zodiac.

In the Chinese zodiac, only some animals get along with other specific animals. As an example, someone with the sign of the dog would get along with someone with a tiger sign. They would search for a person born in the year of the tiger because it states they would get along. It is believed that people born in the year of the dog and tiger have great communication.

Realize, however, that people of the same sign will not necessarily get along, although there is a possibility. Whether a relationship would be successful or not can be determined by using the zodiac.

People who would be planning on getting into something significant, like marriage, and are serious in their belief in Chinese astrology would confer with an astrologer before they would take any action. They would also do the same for people who they would work or be in business with. This also includes forming friendships. There are many people who have used this approach in their lives and still use it today.

Religion

The Chinese calendar is the history of what the zodiac is based on and associated with ancient religion and Chinese astrology. The religion of Taoism is influenced by zodiac. In the beliefs of Taoists, constellations, and space are used to decide a person's "future."

Chinese astrology believes that the position of the things that are in space can have an effect on a person's destiny and applies to the zodiac. The sun was used to determine how all zodiac signs were going to operate according to the dates and times.

Frequently, in many zodiacs, embedded in the center is a yin-yang symbol that represents any two contrasting principles in the universe and how it all works. The religion of Taoism is where the yin-yang originated. It is the well-known symbol of Taoism that believes that "man is a microcosm for the universe."

Yin-Yang

The yin-yang links with the zodiac because it is connected with the Zodiac's five elements to read the ten stems the zodiac uses to count days, months, and years. When it is all combined, the yin-yang affects the 12 zodiac animals and their characteristics.

Buddhism is another example of how religion links with the zodiac. One of the legends in this religion tells how all the animals were chosen for the zodiac by Buddha inviting them.

The majority of people practice Buddhism, which has the greatest religious impact on China and is significantly important to Chinese culture. The structure of the zodiac and what it has become has been influenced by religion.

Other Countries Influenced by the Chinese Zodiac

Many different cultural zodiacs worldwide have been influenced by the Chinese zodiac. Several other countries, principally Asian, were under China and its influence at one time. The Chinese Zodiac has been impactful on zodiacs in the countries of Thailand, Japan, and Vietnam.

The varied zodiacs in these other countries are about the same as the Chinese. However, there are some differences and distinctions. The differences include the selection of animals, signs, and stories of origin.

In the Japanese zodiac, instead of a pig, the zodiac has a wild boar; a cat instead of a rabbit; and instead of a sheep, it has a goat.

In the Vietnamese zodiac, instead of an ox, they have a water buffalo, and in the Thailand zodiac, there is a very large snake, a naga that is in the place of the dragon.

The Chinese Zodiac has had their signs used by many cultures for many various uses other than the zodiac. For example, annual postage stamps celebrating Chinese culture have used the signs. Other uses have been for decoration or tattoos.

The Chinese zodiac has, in many countries, changed the way millions of people view life in association with their beliefs of the Chinese Zodiac.

Mythology — Racing to the Finish

There are many versions of this story. Some say the Jade Emperor wanted to create the Chinese zodiac and called a race of animals on his birthday. There are others who claim that the Buddha did this. Regardless of the details, excluding some minor particulars, the story is basically the same.

As the myth is told, the twelve animals selected for the Chinese zodiac were chosen through a race. Time measurement for the people is the reason that the race was created. In order to win, animals had to reach the finish line on the shore after crossing a rapidly current river. There could only be twelve winners.

The animals that won the race in the order they won were the rat, ox, tiger, rabbit, dragon, horse, snake, monkey, rooster, sheep, dog, and the pig. Some of the animals had unique ways of getting across the river, but they were the animals that won the race. (Washington.edu Staff, 2007)

The lunar calendar follows the outcome of the race, the rat being first and the pig last. Once the lunar calendar gets to the pig, the sequence begins again. The lunar calendar has been an important calendar for China and the Chinese zodiac. There are many parts of the world that recognize this calendar.

Chinese Zodiac

Hinduism Astrology

A very important part of Hinduism is astrology and its part of Vedanga and part of Vedic self-understanding. The Vedic period of knowledge is total science. The Astrology system is part of the ancient Vedic period. (Goravani, 2019)

Vedic Astrology is a reference to Indian or Hindu astrology, a system originating in ancient India and recognized by sages in the Vedic scriptures. It is also known as Jyotish, the science of light. This astrology deals with pattern thought to determine our destiny and future, known as astral light patterns.

The Principle of Vedic Astrology

Astrology is the science of understanding the influence of the sun, moon, stars, and planets upon living creatures. The heavenly bodies, including the planets, have an effect throughout a human being's life, and the planetary effects are "fruit of karma."

The premise of Vedic astrology is that all things are connected. Your fortune or karma is decided by a cosmic design that is predestined. You are a soul, and that soul is manifesting in a body at a very particular place and time.

Your life is a manifestation of a greater whole into which you are born, as, at certain times, flowers bloom when all the circumstances are perfectly agreeable. According to the concept of karma, it is the case with our births on this planet.

The Jyotish is a map of the planets in the signs of the zodiac. Charts are cast based on the exact moment at an exact place on earth. So, the place and moment you were born to create a chart known as your birth chart or natal chart.

Astrologers claim they can know much about you by reading the chart of the heavens for the time and place of your birth. The planets and their positions in the star-based zodiac are taken, and your predictive timeline, known as "dashas," are arranged. The Vedic chart will reveal your real life, and your dashas are probably operating properly.

The Vedic astrologer looks at the signs, planets, and house placements in your chart and can "see" your personality, life events, and possibilities, both the good and the bad events and times in your life. The moments when the events develop in life are determined by the dashas. (Goravani, 2019)

The Predictive Vedic Astrology

A predictive accuracy to Vedic astrology is given by the dashas, which is greater than what is possible with Western astrology. Unique to the Vedic system, the planetary ruling periods give the Vedic astrologers a tool for precisely forecasting the changes, trends, and events in your life with a precision that is nothing short of amazing.

Vedic astrologers can delve more deeply into what's going to happen in your life and less limited to speaking about you in general terms.

Many Vedic astrology practitioners believe that it is a great source of insightful knowledge and offers a means of predicting and understanding the events of life.

Conclusion

Thank you for reading *Astrology Activated: Cutting Edge Insight Into the Ancient Art of Astrology (Understanding Zodiac Signs and Horoscopes)* to the end.

Many people end up not reading through an entire book. The book's title would initially intrigue someone, who then buys the book to read it. But before they can get through the book, a distraction would lead them to put it down and move on to other activities.

It seems that you are interested and serious about learning the art of astrology, your personal Zodiac sign, the effects of the planets on your natal chart, and how it affects your personality and the events in your life.

Before you read this book, you may not have had an inkling on how much you would learn about your birth sign and how the planets affect each sign in your astrological chart or even how to do so.

Reading about your own sign and realizing how closely you identify with its characteristics will give you better insight into how you act and react, how you decide on things, what you should be doing, and what you need to work on yourself.

It is also interesting to learn why people act and react the way they do and how much they resemble the characteristics of their signs as well.

Hopefully, you enjoyed this book and found it informative, guiding you to the art of astrology, the Zodiac, and your horoscope.

Description

Has anyone ever asked you, "What's your sign?" Do you answer them with your Sun sign? Or do you expand their knowledge by telling them not only your Sun sign but also the signs where your Ascendant and Moon are? If you do, that's pretty impressive, but if you don't, read on.

If you want to learn about the art of astrology and what the stars say about your Sun sign and the planets that influence how you act and interact with others, then this book, *Astrology Activated: Cutting Edge Insight Into the Ancient Art of Astrology (Understanding Zodiac Signs and Horoscopes)* is a must-read for you!

Astrology was first created by astronomers in the 18TH Century B.C. in Mesopotamia by the Babylonians. The first astronomers studied astronomy and complemented their studies with astrology.

Astronomers created astrological charts to predict the change in seasons and celestial events that recurred every year. The combination of the astrological charts and the movements of the planets had led them to consider that astronomy and astrology are the same science for 2,000 years.

In astrology, the planets are the most important carriers of the role and destiny of a person's horoscope. Each planet has its own identity and impact of where they are at the time of a person's birth. Your Sun sign is the most prominent because it is the planet that is closest to the sun when you are born.

So many aspects of your birth can be discovered by your natal chart. Physical appearance, constitution, and health, whether you're romantic, pragmatic, mysterious, full of energy, or slow. Also, plodding can be revealed when we learn about our fully drawn astrological chart.

Today, millions of people follow and use astrology for their own purposes, whether they want to have a natal chart drawn for themselves or a member of their family. They may also have their astrology reading drawn twice a year—on their birthday and the new year.

Horoscopes are printed in nearly every newspaper or can be found on a myriad of websites online to follow each day and read by millions. There are some who plan their business dealings or trips abroad around what their horoscope says, while others read it on a casual basis out of curiosity.

Some of the highlights of Astrology Activated are:

- o How the Planets affect the astrological chart and the Zodiac signs

- A review of the 12 signs of the Zodiac and which planet rules each sign
- How a natal chart is drawn, an explanation of the Houses, Zodiac signs, and each element that affects each sign
- Your Sun sign and how it relates to your birth and the characteristics that go with it
- How to determine your Moon sign and your Rising sign
- Find out if your birthdate falls on a cusp and how you're affected by both signs
- Find out if you're reading your horoscope correctly—are you just focusing on your Sun sign?
- And more……

www.ingramcontent.com/pod-product-compliance
Lightning Source LLC
Chambersburg PA
CBHW081752100526
44592CB00015B/2392